"Mr. Obit Voices Death – Now He's Ready to Live"

– Peggy Fletcher Stack, Salt Lake Tribune

"Craig has found obituaries to die for. Many are so compelling I'd like to borrow their deepest regrets and best accomplishments for characters in my next murder mystery."

– Doc Macomber, Author, "The Killer Coin", "Wolf's Remedy", "Snip", "Riff Raff"

"This read made me realize there are many things more regretful than a bad tattoo and nothing better than a good woman and a life well lived."

– Lyle Tuttle, 79, Tattoo Legend and Historian

Have The Last Word – Write Your Own Obituary

(And Learn to Live)

By
Craig C. Dunford

Floating Word Press, LLC
Portland, Oregon

Floating Word Press, LLC
1017 SW Morrison Street, Suite 215
Portland, Oregon 97205

Some names, places and incidents in the obituaries are products of the author's imagination.

All rights reserved, including the right of reproduction in whole or in part in any form.

No part of this publication may be reproduced or transmitted in any form or by any means, electronic or mechanical, including photocopy, recording, or any information storage or retrieval system, without permission in writing from the publisher.

Copyright © 2011 by Craig C. Dunford

Floating Word Press logo is a registered trademark. For information about special discounts for bulk purchases, please contact Floating Word Press, LLC, Special Sales at 1-877-356-9673 or fwp@floatingwordpress.com.

COVER & LAYOUT DESIGNED BY KAT MAJORS GRA-FIX

Editor: Martha Cowen

Author photograph Copyright © 2011 by Craig C. Dunford

Manufactured in the United States of America

Printing Number

10 9 8 7 6 5 4 3 2 1

First Edition

Library of Congress Control Number: 2011933813

Soft Cover: ISBN – 13: 978-0-9785717-1-9

Ebook Edition by Floating Word Press, LLC

*This book is dedicated to Mitzi
for teaching me to tie a knot.*

Have The Last Word – Write Your Own Obituary
(And Learn to Live)

CONTENTS

Preface 1

CHAPTER 1
Writing Your Own Obituary 3

CHAPTER 2
How This Book Came To Be 5

CHAPTER 3
Getting Started 7
    Worksheet 9

CHAPTER 4
Self-Written Obituaries 11

CHAPTER 5
Odds and Ends 83
    Write Your Own Funeral – or as it's called these days
    – Your Celebration of Life 83
    Write Your Own Exit 84
    Shoot Your Own Obituary Photo 90
    Your Final Resting Place 91

CHAPTER 6
Miscellaneous Reflections 103

Conclusion 118

Acknowledgments 120

Related Reading 121

Related Videos 122

Internet 123

PREFACE

To most, obituaries bring to mind a page in the newspaper about the end of lives. Each obituary provides a brief description of the person's statistics. We don't generally like to think about these sad yet often rote third-person descriptions of lost lives, but if we reframe our thought process, it's a page with great potential. Obituaries can contain some of the most interesting, amazing and touching stories imaginable. I know that I am not alone when it comes to being drawn to this subject. One first-person obituary in particular inspired me to write my own. Over time, I became more immersed in this subject, attending conferences, reading and viewing everything I could about death and dying. I discovered that health care professionals in the hospice field seemed "different" when compared to their counterparts in other medical areas. They seemed calmer, more caring, and centered in their lives. It occurred to me that being near those who are dying could change you in very positive way. The fabric of these lives appears to become thicker, richer. Not all, but many seem to strip away the inconsequential things. There are no pretenses, no games, and they have great enthusiasm for the life that is here now. This clarity of thought is so compelling that it is not unusual for caregivers to fall in love with someone near death. I found that there is much to be learned from those who feel they are close to death and from their caregivers.

As I read obituary pages, one of several things struck me besides the various ages at which people die. Death came to some so unexpectedly. Not many people actually know when they are going to die. But those that do have a tendency to live a more real, vital and honest life near the end. It is to our advantage to live each day as if it was the last. I understand I am not the first one to promote this idea. Hollywood has even made a movie about this subject, "The Bucket List", and country singer, Tim McGraw, had a hit with the song, "Live Like You Were Dying". Since it is observable to me that most of us don't live this way, I felt we could use a tool to achieve this goal. The tool I found was writing my own obituary.

Not only was it helpful to me personally, but it also became a significant life exercise in all of the cases where I helped someone else.

I consider myself to be an ordinary guy. I grew up in an ordinary family, in a conservative city and state. I, like most, wanted to work in my family's business, get married, have a child or two, watch some TV, and live happily ever after. For me, to be writing something like this is, to say the least, unusual. Something quite powerful has happened to me. It seems reasonable to me that if this experience could positively impact me, it might do the same for other seekers.

Chapter 1 consists of suggestions for getting started, things to think about. Chapter 2 describes what started this whole affair and contains the obituary that began this journey. To insure privacy, names and some facts have been changed. Chapter 3 is a workbook. Space is provided to use this section as a workbook. You might want to keep this book handy to record thoughts as they come to you.

Chapter 4 contains my observations and examples of the themes of self-written obituaries, beginning with obituaries by my own family.

Chapter 5 has all the extraneous odds and ends you might consider when you decide to "Have the Last Word" and Chapter 6 contains others' reflections on this subject.

We're all floating in the bathtub of life. Problem is, we don't know how close we are to the drain. Make the most of it while you are still afloat. To those who find this subject as fascinating as I do, I'd appreciate hearing from you about your particular interest and observations. If you choose to "write your own" I would be honored if you would send me a copy of your obituary.

My address is: craigdunford@yahoo.com.
Twitter me at: mrobituary.

Remember, it's about living.

Craig

CHAPTER 1
Writing Your Own Obituary

We peruse other people's obituaries in the newspaper. But we try not to think about our own. For most, the concept of our own death is too troublesome. However, years ago, I came across an obituary that had been written by the deceased person herself before her death. (I discuss this further in Chapter 2.) In this obituary, I saw a story of life, not death. At that time, the idea to do the same for myself was born. This concept may seem unusual, because we don't generally feel the presence of death. I'm guessing she felt it.

How many of us know when we will die? Would you want to know when it is your time? Do you think addressing our finiteness will hasten the end? What is it about not looking at our own death that makes us feel safer? Which are we more afraid of, dying or living?

The experience of writing my own obituary was very helpful in that it turned my attention to these difficult questions. Looking at what I'd learned crystallized thoughts about the meaning of my life, and identifying what was valuable to me. Writing my obituary also provided me with the opportunity to say what I wanted to say to those I love before it was too late. Furthermore, I feel that by creating my own obituary, I've lightened the load of friends and loved ones I'll leave behind. Of course, this doesn't mean they can't add to what I've written, but they won't have to be concerned that my wishes be conveyed. I see an obituary as a living document, one that changes and grows as you do.

As humans, we have a unique opportunity. We can contemplate why we are here. I believe anyone who tries writing his or her own obituary will derive a positive experience from it. In my observations of obituaries over the years I have discovered certain themes. Generally, these themes describe the type of person this was, i.e. young, old, well educated, hard worker, mother, etc. I have included these obituaries, as an aid to you in your writing. You may see yourself fitting into one of these themes. It may also be helpful to see how others perceived these people. I believe it is sometimes of great value for someone else to write a person's obituary (and you will also see examples of that in this book) because sometimes they know the person better than they know themselves.

CHAPTER 2
How This Book Came To Be

I hadn't really given much thought to obituaries until late 1991 when I missed the funeral of an old friend. Afterward I began to pay more attention to that section of the paper. One evening I came across an obituary self-written by Cheryl McInich Defa. I remember sitting at the dining room table with tears streaming down my face. I was amazed at how this woman's words touched me and how much I learned from them. Below is the obituary that inspired me to pursue this project:

Cheryl McInich Defa

"I died today, January 11, 1992 at the age of 38. Awfully young, don't you think? The culprit was breast cancer that had spread to my lungs. I fought hard for two years with the help of a great medical staff and terrific support from my friends who kept my spirits up, but cancer finally won.

I thank my parents for a great childhood, growing up on the coast of Maine. Your love, devotion, and support when I decided to leave home and see the West gave me strength throughout my life. Thanks also for all the love and support from my sister Charlene and brother-in-law Steven Bishop. I married Guy Defa, the greatest, and most caring, gentle, compassionate man on earth. I only wish we had met sooner, so we would have had more time together. Our five years together were the best. I love you. I'll miss you. I'm going off on the ultimate adventure (and maybe earn a new merit badge). GOOD BYE!

In lieu of donations, please send flowers, as I've already made my contribution to the Cancer Society and besides flowers are much prettier. Please no viewing, no funeral, and no black.

Instead, a celebration of life on Saturday, 12 Noon, January 18, 1992, at the Wasatch Lawn Mortuary Chapel, 3401 S. Highland Drive. Please plant a pink tulip for me. Thanks and good-bye and I'll miss everyone! Beam Me Up Scotty!"

Feeling the strength and beauty of her relationships helped me reevaluate my own. It forced me to think about what I considered truly important in my life. Her sense of humor helped ease my own fear of dying. Reading her words led me to believe that if more people wrote their own obituaries, we would all benefit beyond our comprehension. Thank you Cheryl.

I continued to read obituaries, and observed that most contained little information beyond the deceased's birthplace and date, marital status, a list of survivors, and instructions on how to get to the funeral. To me, this was a waste of a precious opportunity. What better place to say who you were, what you learned in this life, and to express one last message to those left behind? I cannot think of a better medium for human connection. A friend of mine once pointed out that one of the greatest gifts we can give to one another is the sharing of our true selves. Writing our own obituary is a means of offering such a gift.

I believe that in most cases you best write the essence of your life.

Thus, I wrote my own. To my surprise, during this process, the view of what I wanted out of my life became clearer. I realized that anyone else writing my obituary wouldn't have known the things I wanted to say. I discovered that writing about what is important in my life allowed me to make a comparison with what I'm actually doing, and helps me to "stay on track" and actually live up to my words. It also makes me realize the value of each day, each moment.

It occurred to me that, for a myriad of reasons, those left after one dies may not want, or be capable of telling your "true" story. Writing one's own obituary can help ensure that the truth of your life be known.

CHAPTER 3
Getting Started

"I do not write to survive my mortal self, but being alive and full of curious thoughts today, it pleases me to say 'this book, when I am dead, will be a little faint perfume of me.'" Edna St. Vincent Millay

My advice is to be in a quiet calm place. You may want to travel to a special "retreat," (i.e., beach, mountains, desert, etc.). Surround yourself with your books, photos, and any memorabilia you have collected up to this point in your life. Then, observe these things one at a time. Make a list of what you see. Ask yourself "What part does this particular item play in my life?", or "What does this remind me of?"

For example, looking around me I see the following: golf equipment – bakery books and recipes – many "how to" books – woodworking tools, crafts, projects – motorcycles – audio books – computer – intimate memorabilia and souvenirs (misc. books, feathers, stones, letters, candles, etc.) – mementos of being a dad, husband, relative, and friend.

You might want to first jot down a few thoughts about each subject. For instance, "nothing drove me crazier than the game of golf". Then, start to eliminate the least important things by asking:

What do I most want people to know about me? What is the best advice I can offer my survivors? What are the most important things I have to say to my family/friends?

It is said that Ernest Hemmingway had several writing "tricks". For example, before engaging in his favorite activity, libation at social clubs, he required of himself at least one written sentence. He also never wrote all the way to the end of an idea; he left some of it in the cupboard, so to speak, for tomorrow.

We all lead busy lives and time is at a premium for many. My advice is to make a specific written appointment with yourself to write and think. You don't have to do this all at one time. Once a week for a month, or a year might work for you. Early in the morning before anyone else is up, or after everyone is in bed. A short walk on your afternoon break with a notebook for jotting down ideas might be the ticket.

The following is a list of questions I asked myself before I actually began writing my obituary. You might find these helpful:

What are my earliest memories of life?

What do I want to say about my life?

What do I want to say to my family and friends? What will truly touch them?

Do I have any regrets?

What have I received from or given to the world?

What have I learned from life?

What was the cause of my death? (In cases of long illnesses)

Who would I like to thank?

What comfort can I offer my survivors?

What advice do I have for them?

What special instructions do I have for my funeral, viewing, wake?

WORKSHEET

You may find this worksheet helpful for organizing your thoughts before writing the actual obituary.

MY NAME IS

I WAS BORN (DATE/PLACE)

CLOSE FAMILY MEMBERS WERE

MY CHILDHOOD WAS

MY LIFE HERE HAS A PURPOSE. I BELIEVE IT IS

BEFORE I DIE I WOULD LIKE TO

THUS FAR IN MY LIFE, I HAVE LEARNED

ABOUT ME AND MY LIFE I'D LIKE TO UNDERSTAND

I REGRET THAT

I'D LIKE TO TELL
(Name)   THAT

(Name)   THAT

I WAS HAPPY THAT

I WAS SAD THAT

I WAS AFRAID THAT

I HOPE THAT

I'M PROUD THAT

IN MY FINAL DAYS I'D LIKE

I'D LIKE MY FUNERAL TO BE

I'D LIKE TO THANK

DATE

Keep in mind your answers to some of the above questions may change. What's important to you today may not be in two years, two months, or two days. For this reason you may want to date your comments. Remember, this is not a static document. It is as alive and changing as you are.

CHAPTER 4
Self-Written Obituaries

Here are some examples of self-written obituaries by the still living, who also happen to be members of my family. I have discovered that it is sometimes tough to live up to my dead "persona". My comments are in italics.

One of the more powerful experiences I've had since this whole thing started was the day my sister, my wife and I spent on a secluded beach in Hawaii. The day was meant to be "obituary writing day".

Jayne Dunford

"Today I died. My life was about school. I always felt like a beginner at some aspect that I wanted to master. I was sure I could master anything early on. Later I began to see limits in my time, and in my physical energy. The other half of learning is teaching. So, I began to think of sharing what I knew. This taught me everything is one. Teaching is learning and learning is teaching– endlessly moving toward perfection never reached. I think that is how being human felt to me.

I'm happy I lived past the raging hormonal stage of puberty where ancient unnamed wants and desires flooded my body and created a war in my civilized mind that could have no winner. Bad girl – Good girl: I couldn't find the balance. It felt like the only recourse was the peace of suicide. I stayed with the blizzard of frenzied feelings till I could name my demons and eventually tame them through a growing love of my humanity. My budding acceptance of self opened the door to an acceptance of others and acceptance of unspeakable holiness pervading us all and the universe we inhabit.

I don't know where "I" go now that I have died. But I've felt the pervading force of divine love and forgiveness pass through me and yet be who I am too; so I feel in some way infinite. I am at peace as I write today. I am the wind, the sun, the thorns, and the breath of life. I am the student and the teacher and the infinite.

I thank all those who were real with me from my childhood on: those who had the courage to speak their truth and those who could listen without blame or judgment.

This is what I'd like to pass on although I can't name the source of it.
1. Show up.
2. Pay attention to what has heart and meaning.
3. Tell the truth without blame or judgment.
4. Be open to outcome, not attached to outcome.

I always liked things measured and counted and numbered and weighed as though that was the real order of things. Living with an order my mind couldn't wrap itself around was problematic to me. I always tried to look under the accounting at what counted really. But, I feel I have far to go. I was a good counter and measurer though and I loved putting order and my own aesthetic grace in all my environments.

I enjoyed beauty in every form and eventually I even learned to think my own body was a lovely, beautiful, and sexy woman. I loved dressing up and dressing up my family and friends. It made me feel I could be all sorts of unlimited selves with just the change of an outfit. I supposed I felt I'd outwitted time and energy. I was fortunate to be able to indulge my passion for dress up because I could buy lots of fun costumes and began to trade with treasured family members and friends. I learned that wearing a treasured comrade's shirt carried all their hopes and dreams and fantasies too. Wearing clothes became holy to me. Wearing Zuni's shirt kept her alive in my heart and she continued to be a teacher to me long after her death. I've passed clothing on to special people who touched my life. This time they really are a gift and I won't ask for them back if you don't wear them."

My wife, Mitzi, has written two obituaries, one public and the other private.

Miriam Dunford

"This time I'm not exaggerating...

No "tall tales" or "Mitzisms" as you have called them. I died... really died on the___day of____in this____year.

To my loving and supportive family and friends I say thank you. Thank you for being my teachers and students.

To all the second graders whose lives I touched, know that you also touched mine.

To all the little ones at the Children's Centers,

To the hundreds of clients who trusted me enough to go on your journeys and invited me to join you,

I say thank you.

I lived. I really lived. Capturing the magic in the "ordinary" embracing the light and the shadow."

❧

Craig C. Dunford

(Updated April 2011)

"Everybody dies, but not everybody lives." Dr. J. Healey

5/22/42 to _____.

"A few days ago I died.

I knew it would happen, just not when. Yet, here I am with all the other wonderful people on this page, physically gone. I had a superb life there, and was fortunate to have loving parents, siblings, wife, children, friends and business associates. There is a special place in my heart for my excellent pallbearers: Alyce, Julie, Mary Jane, Marjorie, Matty, Sally, and Tamara. We had a lot of fun getting ready.

To those nearest me, I hope I have not waited to tell you how much I love you. If I didn't tell you yesterday, then I'll tell you now: I LOVE YOU today and will again tomorrow.

I've thought for some time that all I really wanted from life was to feel valuable. I got that feeling; not from things, but from experiences with the above-mentioned people. Only two people really know how truly amazing and wonderful my life with Mitzi was. In my humble opinion, we ended up with great children. I'm proud of you Erin and Miles.

I hope I learn as much here as I did there. Such as:

Enjoy the journey! Live in the authentic present (Thoreau)

Writing your own obituary is a valuable and rewarding experience (CD)

Embrace what frightens you and "let go of the peanuts" (??) *I'll tell you that story someday.*

Follow your bliss (JC)

Who do you expect to please with that little thing? (BR)

We all have light and shadow (RJ)

Being real is more important than being right (JD)

Don't make it ordinary (CD)

Few things are sweeter than a crisp 3 wood over all the trouble for all the money (Jeremy)

That being said, I truly disliked playing golf for money (CD)

To value my own judgment – receive input, but the final decision is mine (CD)

Life is not a dress rehearsal (TS)

Best web site to save the world: TED.com (TED)

When we resort to violence, it becomes obvious we have not progressed very far (CD)

What we are pretending not to know (Lifespring)

Live in love and harmlessness (TD)

It's what YOU DO with what happens that REALLY matters (Epictitus)

Keep your word. It's actually the most valuable thing you possess. I think you do take it with you (Lifespring)

I never liked yard work, and wondered if God knew which plants were weeds (I'll ask) (CD)

One accomplishment gave me a feeling of value above all else: That I could be the wind beneath my best friend's wings (MD)

To my family and friends: It's OK to have pain, as I did when loved ones left me, but hanging on to the pain will not be helpful to you or me.

When you smile, laugh, drink a beer, or miss a two-foot putt, I am there.

"Love does not die, people do. So when all that is left of me is Love, Give me away." I don't know who wrote this, but I like it very much.

To all of those who still have a bamboo cup, please bring them to the "party after the party". Let's see if they still hold liquid. You were a big part of my life.

LOVE, Craig"

You don't have to be "eccentric" to write your own obituary. Each person will have his or her own reasons and benefits for doing this. My mom likes having things in order. This is a perfect reflection of her life, though she might have to update the great and great great grandchildren part.

Mae Dunford

"I was born on a wintry day, Dec. 28, 1914, in Richfield, Utah to the best parents one could ask for, John and Francetty Christensen, who taught me and my six brothers and sisters the principles of life that would ensure happy, healthy and successful lives. My marriage to Stephen Love Dunford in the Salt Lake L.D.S. temple assured me of his continued love in the life beyond. Our seven children brought to me the challenges and love that make life worth living – each in his or her own way. My hope is for my children, Larry, Craig, Jayne, Kay, Jim, Steven and Chris and their spouses, Janice, Mitzi, Steve Lovell,

Sharon Dunford, and my eight grandchildren, and 17.5 great grandchildren, and .5 great great grandchild to remember the good things they have learned from my example, and to forget the mistakes I made along the way – or learn by them. The opportunities I have had to participate in church activities and to associate with members have filled many hours that would have been lonely."

Maybe the most significant Christmas gift I ever received from my daughter:

Erin Dunford

"So today I died.

Today I am transformed, and I move on... I believe in the theory of "Not Knowing". I don't know what I'm doing dead, and I didn't know what I was doing (most of the time) when I was alive. I especially don't know what I'm doing writing these words! But here goes! This is what remains:

What a strange brilliant, brief moment my life was. I died dreaming... loved dreaming... it was hard for me to love the "here & now". My life, my feelings, my dreams were changing always... minute by minute... change was the one thing I found to be absolute... none of us are immune to it...

I loved to learn... and the power of words amazed me. I was often afraid to learn about myself.

I thrived on stress. I was young and strong, but I was not unbreakable – not perfect. Who would want to be?

I loved my family (a lot!) often I was my own best friend, yet my family was there no matter what! Thank you! I love you! I loved order, but I learned that life goes on in disorder and sometimes chaos fuels the most amazing things! I loved independence. At age 5, 10, 14, or 18 I loved the sense that I could do anything I wanted to do! I was able to bring to life my own dreams... I loved to write! Despite the fact that it always scared me just a bit. Despite the countless nights in front of the computer and all the bitching, my words are my own, and they are powerful.

I want you all to know what made me happy in this life... so here are a few glimpses into my bliss:

Cold Utah nights under a toasty electric blanket. Reading with mom.

Both of the Mandys: the doll and the imaginary friend

The Blankie – the eternal symbol of my inner self. Porch swings

Kindergarten. Dressing up (from age three on). Make over days

Long baths, with a different soap for every part of the body;

Homemade facials and painted toe nails

Good books, suntan lotion, summer days and big back yards

Bats! (They're not just for Halloween any more)

Being crazy with dad: i.e. road trips to Idaho, dangerous expeditions, remote control, fish (and countless others!)

High school road trips: concerts, debate, friends and Dunhill cigarettes.

Coffee (or "going to" coffee). Conversation and laughs. Spontaneous camping trips

School supplies. Being done with finals. Christmas mornings with my family (even minus presents and tree, it would be great if they were there)

Having someone I really love hold me and tell me how much they care.

Eating hot French bread with your fingers. a kick ass workout in self-defense class. Chill mornings

So that was life huh? Pretty amazing!

This obituary certainly doesn't say it all, but it can't, I suppose. Don't mourn me with tears and black garb, please do celebrate my life. You will only mourn because death is a scary thing. Do not worry about me. I will be fine. Instead, embrace the shadow and call it your own and plunge into the unknown – it's the best way to live and die… 'til next time. Erin"

The following are obituaries written by older individuals who lived a very long time and died of age-related conditions. There is a different tone in these obituaries that reflects lives well lived, whether capturing it in a fully detailed description or with just a line or two.

Mike Herd

"Happy Wednesday, my friends. I began this wonderful journey called life on Aug. 22, 1920. I was born to Donna and Phil Herd in the small mining town of Array, Utah. Later I was to be joined by sister, Laura, and brother, Harold. Carol and I met and married in Jan. 1944, and had two beautiful children; James and Ronnie, who have been my best friends, especially after Carol died in 1988. I worked for many years in the automobile industry and enjoyed my 28 years with Smith Ford. The people I met there became special friends and I thank them for the time we shared together. What an exciting adventure my life has been. I was never quite able to perfect my golf swing while here and so, on Saturday, December 10, 1990, while sitting comfortably in my chair, I went in search of my swing, a new golf course and to rejoin my little honey I hope each and every one of you stops to take the time and enjoy your own special journeys through life. Farewell and God Bless... Mike."

꙳

Spence Granger

"I was born the year Utah was made a state. I was the oldest child in our family. I remember the first automobile to come to Heber. Not many people paid the 5 cents to ride it because it would never last."

꙳

Sheldon Harper Holmes
"Loving Father"

"I was born December 19, 1918 in Harper Ward, Utah, son of Delbert Samuel Holmes and Sarah Abby Harper. I was preceded in death by my Sweetheart, Ila, granddaughter; parents, two brothers and one sister. I grew up in a family of six children of whom Clinton (Eris) Holmes, Alice (Owen) Brough survive. I was educated in Brigham City, attending Box Elder High School, where I met my sweetheart, Ila. We were married September 8, 1938; the marriage was solemnized September 8, 1943 in the Logan Temple. I served my country in the US Navy, several community governing boards, and the LDS Church. My greatest blessings and assets were my wife, Ila; my children: Douglas (Nan) Holmes, Sydney Christensen, Julie Kent, Kirk (Patsy) Holmes; seven grandchildren and ten great-grandchildren. Life has been a great journey. I have lived during the greatest time in history and saw so many great advancements in technology. The greatest need I see is for love of one another and peace in the world. I pray for these blessings to happen. The family would like to extend a special thanks to Superior Home Care Hospice. Funeral services will be held Wednesday, 11:00 a.m. at the Granger 18th Ward, 2850 West 3835 South. A viewing will be held Tuesday, 6- 8:00 p.m. at McDougal Funeral Home, 4330 South Redwood Road and Wednesday at the church, 10- 10:45 a.m. Interment, Valley View Memorial Park. In lieu of flowers donations may be made to The Deseret Foundation."

❧

Delmar Leo Kenney

"Hi, my name is Delmar Leo Kenney I have nine children and each of you knows who you are. You have blessed me with many grandkids and even more great grandkids, all of whom I love. If I had to live this life over, I would change a couple of things. One: I would have stayed with the woman I still love more than anything in the world, Catherine. Two: I would like to have spent a lot more time with each of my kids. Please forgive me. I love you all. I became very tired and sickly over the past little while, and I am glad that I was called back home on November 14, 2003. Ya know it's great up here. The meadow grass is belly high, and the streams are the clearest I've ever looked into. I've been given a string of horses to take care of. Some are good sound horses while others I am going to have to break. My body is working well now, so I shouldn't have any problem with the work ahead of me. I won't keep you any longer, besides I have to get started. Know I love you all and am glad that I got to have you as family and friends. Until we meet again, know that God loves you. Delmar."

Wendy Biers

"I, Wendy Biers danced off to Paradise in great joy on January 22, 1994. I was born by lamplight on May 1, 1935 in a little log cabin on Lamb Creek, just above Camille Springs in Nevada, to Will and Mona Jones. I ran a private school for over 10 years, which presented the opportunity to see the great good in so many people and created throughout my life the larger opportunity for the expression of love. My "skinny little body" will be buried Nov. 22 at Norris Mortuary. My last request to you is that you will make the effort to see the good in others. I'd like you to remember to praise God, especially in your infirmities. The last words I want you to hear me saying are, "Thank you to you and thank you to Jesus.""

Terri Simons

"I was born 1928 youngest of 10. I married my childhood sweetheart. We started our family, which has grown from five children to 19 grandchildren, 40 great-grandchildren, and eight great great grandchildren. When your hour comes, walk toward the light and I will be waiting with open arms."

Phyllis Dunnigan

"Together Again" I was born at home weighing two and a half pounds at the Constitution Building on Main Street in Salt Lake City, Utah. My dad taught me to tap dance and I performed at age six at the Salt Lake Theater. I enjoyed dancing my entire life and as a young adult planned dances for the World War II service men at Ft. Douglas and Memory Grove. As a child I lived in Delta (80 acre farm), Santa Ana, CA, Brigham City, and Salt Lake City. Growing up I loved to swim and enjoyed teaching and competing in swimming. My father and mother were both very spiritual and taught me to love the gospel of Jesus Christ. I graduated from West High and held various jobs including working as an accountant for Salt Lake County Health Department. I have a deep love for the Savior. I loved the youth and enjoyed serving in many church callings and researching family history. I loved to travel and I especially loved cruises with my family. I met my husband to be, George B. Dunnigan, when he worked as a MP at Fort Douglas. I asked him out, gave him a big red apple, and beat him on our tennis date."

Alice Sprig Davis Allen

"My birth in England brought great joy to my parents and grandparents who thought I was the prettiest baby in town. My family and I survived World War II and the years spent as refugees. During my teens, we lived near the North Sea, the greatest place in which to grow up. In 1955 I came to Ogden. A year later I helped my family come over. I married my girlhood sweetheart after helping him come to the U.S. as well. I had two children with him. The marriage ended nine years later.

In 1968 I married William Davis. I became widowed 5 years later. His gift to me – a lovely daughter. Her presence in my life kept me going.

On April 1, 1976, I married Skip Allen. He adopted my little girl and became a wonderful father to her. We have had 16 great years together. Skip brought contentment and laughter into my life. I have enjoyed extremely good health and never thought I would be the first to go, but that's life. I'm grateful for the pleasure of getting to see my first three grandchildren, all born last year within a few months of each other.

I would like to thank the Allen family for taking me in so graciously. I was fortunate to be loved by those who chose to get to know me and who mattered in my life. Also, I was fortunate to be able to dance ballet until age 40, explore photography, ski with abandon, golf with enthusiasm and paint with delight."

Barbara L. Murdoch

"I was born August 29, 1920 and grew up in Long Island, New York. I had three sons, all good boys that made me proud. I was a kind and gentle woman. I did my best to lead a good life and be the best person I could be, but some days were harder than others.

I loved to sing, read, listen to opera, sew, and much to the disbelief of my youngest son, watch golf on TV. I was also a pretty good cook and I felt complete watching my boys eat. I had a smile for everyone, and despite some hardships, I am thankful for all the friends and family that I had. I died on June 6, 2009. Enjoy your life, smile and laugh."

B. Austin Haws

"I'm writing this obituary myself on 21 April 1997 with a few blanks to be filled in. I'm doing this because I know me better than anyone else and I don't have to look up a lot of information while the mortician is pushing to get my obit. Byron Austin Haws died 29 May 2002 at Sunshine Terrace in Logan at age 80. At this time I know something you don't – what it's like to be dead – and you know something I don't – how I died. But I don't want any of this "poor grandpa" stuff written about me! I've had a great life and I'm ready for the next step."

Glenda Lenore Thornblad Owen
"Together Again"

"I am writing this 14 January 2001. I read the obituaries in the paper and some are SO LONG and others don't give the genealogical information that I feel someone might be looking for. So, after thinking about my age, health, etc., I decided to write what I want in my obituary when the time comes.

I was born 21 January 1919 in Holden, Utah and given the name Glenda Lenore Thornblad. I was the oldest of three children born to Hazel Annie Stephenson and Wilford Torgny

Thornblad. My two brothers were Marvin Wilford (Betty) Thornblad and Warren Bruce (Beverly) Thornblad.

I married Donald Fillmore Owen 23 December 1941 in Oakland, California. We were blessed with five children: Gary Wilford (Joanne), William Henry (Barbara), Nancy Ann (Lawrence) Lords, Irene Elaine (Randy) Lytle and Robert Donald (Carma). These five children have given us 23 grandchildren, who have given us 35 great grandchildren. My husband, Donald and my younger brother Warren preceded me in death.

On 13 April 2004 I left this world peacefully to join my husband and will be buried with him at the Ft. Douglas Cemetery." Glenda's family feels a need to add that she will be remembered for her special love for animals and young children. Her friends span all ages and species."

༄

Robert Douglas Johnson

"My ancestors were all Utah pioneers. My two grandmothers came with the Martin and Robinson Handcart Companies. Died December 9, 2005 of causes incident to age I lived my entire life in Salt Lake City, moving to Holladay, Utah in 1965 and then to Bountiful in 2003 to be near my daughter and her family. I attended local schools, LDS High School, and graduated from LDS Business College in 1932. After graduating from school I met the love of my life, Lillian Sedgeley. We were married in the Salt Lake Temple August 1, 1936. I worked for several companies, joining US Steel Corp in 1946. I worked there for 31 years as a Sales Representative, retiring in 1977."

༄

Dr. Wallace Jay Morgan

"Sometime down the road a doctor is going to declare that I am no longer among the living. I would like to say just a word for the record. People say the darnedest things after you die. They say it most the time in hopes it will come true.

I grew up in Riverton, Utah and on my dad's sheep ranch in Idaho. I loved being a sheepherder. We rode horses, shot bear, shot at coyotes, chopped wood, made fences and lived in tents on the high rugged mountains of the Caribou National Forest. We ate venison, sage hens, grouse, pine hens, sour dough bread, and mutton – all cooked usually on an open fire. It was hard work, interesting, sometimes lonely, but to this day, cherished memories.

It was a wonderful happy childhood with loving parents and older brothers and sisters to look after me. I was the youngest of six children. Sarah, my mother, provided warmth and welcomed all six children and their many friends. Our house was always filled with friends and neighbors. My mother was a wonderful person to grow up with. My father provided the space for this to happen. I was very secure and knew that I was loved.

High school was a marvelous time for me. My schoolmates at Jordon High School allowed me to be president of our class, captain of our football team and captain of our basketball team. We won state championships. It was a wonderful time. I thought I was ten feet tall and bullet proof. After a tour of duty during World War II in the U.S. Navy, I returned to my education.

During the next eight years I studied hard and worked my way through the University of Utah and ended up with a DDS degree from Washington University at St. Louis, MO. For over forty years I've loved and practiced dentistry. I've enjoyed working for so many wonderful and loyal patients.

Married in 1950 and helped raise five children. I divorced after over 30 years of marriage. After ten years of single life and dating several women, (none of whom I wanted to marry) I met a wonderful girl, Janis Murphy Souter, from Ogden. After the first night we met I knew I would marry her. I thought then she was the most beautiful, charming, and most fun–loving, kind person I'd ever met. Together our love returned me to the joy and happiness I had known during my childhood and youth. Our bond was special. I do hope that Janis' belief that there is something after this life is true. It would be very special to spend more time with her. For me, though there seems to be a space between what is and what we want to believe.

I beg forgiveness for those whom I offended during my lifetime and forgive those who have offended me." Wally wanted a celebration of his life to be held at Willow Creek Country Club."

※

Sometimes you have the last word and sometimes you don't. This man knew it and allowed his wife to rewrite his obituary, as she knew him better than he knew himself.

Melvin Keith Pendleton
"Drummin' Man"

"Although having written my obituary years ago, devoting hours to meticulous chronological detail and serious tone, I have learned that compromise with my wife of 57 years, Ellie Pendleton, is never-ending – as is my love for her. With that said, you are not looking at the obituary – appropriate photo that I attached to the draft of the lengthy obituary that you will not read today. Rather, I imagine that Ellie, whom I met on December 7, 1950 – a day of infamy, as I often said – has elected to utilize the picture of me playing the drums in my band days (I was a talented drummer in my day). Keep all of this in mind, as you read the summary and interpretation of my life from my fun loving, risk-taking love of my life. Okay, Ellie, it's all yours."

"The beats of his drum are silent now, and his watercolor brushes are neatly put away. Keith, at the age of 88, has passed on to be united with family and friends. While here on earth, he married Ellie Dean Warren on April 30, 1951 in the Salt Lake Temple, and believe it or not, it lasted 57 years.

Keith was a devoted member of The Church of Jesus Christ of Latter- day Saints. As a young man, he was called to serve in the Spanish-American mission, which at the time extended from Texas to California. He held many positions in the church, but his favorite was that of Home Teacher.

"Ellie, aren't you going to say something about my career? After all, I wrote down five pages on that alone." Keith's professional endeavors in marketing, advertising, and art preceded 35 years of employer relations and vocations with the State of Utah, from which he retired.

"Ellie, can I get one final word in? I want to express gratitude for how much I have been given in my life. Despite serious health oppositions that threatened my existence, I was miraculously preserved to enjoy a full life through God's grace and supportive companionship from a loving family." He shall be greatly missed by all of his family and friends. How fortunate he was to have had so many who dearly loved him. So, until we meet again, we shall hold you close to our hearts. You hold the beat until we get there...

Becky Marks

I hated to leave, but I had a magnificent life. It started in Georgia with the sweetest parents in the world. Our neighbor, after observing our family household for a number of years commented, "I'm sure that's what Heaven will be like."

My brothers and sisters have always meant so much to me. They're dear and special human beings. I attended Baconton (GA) High School and graduated from Huntingdon College (AL) with a Bachelor of Art Degree and a teacher's certificate (which was utilized later). I majored in English and had minors in French and Art.

Married my devoted career Army officer husband, Bob (who preceded me in death), in Coral Gables, Florida, when he returned from the Korean War. We had an exciting life together, traveling and living in fascinating places at home and abroad.

The two most valued treasures in my life of which I was most proud were my beautiful children, Robert Jr. and Lisa. They gave me more pleasure, comfort and joy than I could have possibly imagined. I don't know how I could have been so incredibly lucky. Later after they were married to wonderful

Diane and Kent, I had the privilege of enjoying three adorable grandchildren: Lauren, Easton and Anne. I loved taking them to the ballet, the theatre and going on trips to faraway places.

Retiring in Salt Lake City brought much happiness, spectacular scenery, wonderful friends and neighbors. Our special group goes back to the early seventies when we belonged to various organizations including the Symphony and Ballet Guilds. Our birthday celebrations were a joy, and much anticipated. Bonds were formed that grew stronger through the years.

Friends from Gourmet Club went back a long way too. And what a highlight the Saturday Night Dance Club was. A most rewarding experience was joining the docent program at the Utah Museum of Fine Arts. I received my twenty-year service award in 1996. Sharing my love of art with school children and others was very rewarding. I was a member of the First Presbyterian Church. It was a place for worshipping, learning and wonderful support. I was so grateful."

Many individual's lives revolved around love of family, with all its joys and painful regrets for which they address with humble clarity.

Emily Johansen Pia Apking

"She tried but she died." (Dorothy Parker cynicism) I was born May 29, 1947 to Amy and Clarence Johansen. I died on March 29 of 2009. My incredibly beautiful family survives me. My husband Robert Apking, my children, Sonia Pia and Nick Pia and grandsons, Taylor, Chance and Logan Pia. I'm going to be cremated and there will not be a service. If my family chooses to have a party, that's great, but if not, please give my family a call from time to time. They are going to miss me. Life has been so fun. I hope death is a close second."

Tylor Blane

"On May 19, 1994 I reluctantly left my cherished family, relatives and friends. I leave many memories of good times and bad, the great love we have for each other and the close family relations that were the joy of my life. I loved our family get-togethers and our camping, bowling, and working together as a family. Thanks so much for helping me with all the little odds and ends. I'm so proud of the talents and abilities of each one of you. You are a great family. Thanks for the love you gave to me and remember you were loved as much in return. Thanks too for the lovely grandchildren you blessed me with – each is so dear to me."

Tamara Kim Bumgarner Hook
"Live Well, Love Much, Laugh Often!"

"I was born April 3, 1962 to Robert H. Bumgarner Jr. and Lexie May Updyke Bumgarner. My parents later divorced and both got remarried. I married my high school friend, Russell Layne Hook on June 18, 1981 (later divorced after 23 years of marriage). Together we have two wonderful sons Tyler Layne Hook and Chase Ryan Hook. Both have brought my life utter joy and a sense of purpose.

My favorite things in this life have been my boys, fireworks, dolphins, family, the ocean and a good movie (I was always up for a good movie). This life has been an adventure. Now it is time to rest. I leave behind my beautiful sons, Tyler (his wife Shannon) and Chase. Family: mother; Lexie Spencer, step-father; Spence, stepmother; Donna Bumgarner, brothers; Steve, Kevin, Robbie, sister; Tanya, grandmother Mabel Bumgarner and extended family (too many to name each). My best friends Jeff (Gabe), Shelly, Lynn and so many people that have made me smile during the journey. Thank you. A special thanks to my ex-in-laws who put up with me for so many years. I never stopped caring about you and I missed having you in my life."

Paul Brophy
My Report

"Already it is time to depart, for me to die, for you to go on living. Which of us takes the better course is not known to anyone but God." (Socrates) Father, I have returned to report a most fabulous trip. Nothing has brought me more joy than my stay on Earth. The family I shared and the people I met while there brought me my greatest happiness.

I met, married and shared my life with a most wonderful girl, Sherry Stewart Brophy. She was my greatest source of joy, strength and love while there and I can only hope that we will be united together once again forever. We were blessed to have shared with you six great and noble spirits as our children on Earth. I will be so glad to see them, their eternal companions and their special children. You know, grandchildren are one of your greatest creations you blessed us with during our stay. I am so grateful to you for your gift to us of eternal families. While there I tried to serve you, my family, my church, my country, and my fellowman the best I could."

※

Toni Richmond Spriggs

"Hey those better not be tears I see or sobs I hear. I have had such a wonderful life I don't regret a minute of it. Thank you everyone. I was born May 28, 1952 to Kenneth (Buddy) Richmond, and Cleah McKoween Richmond, the most adoring and loving parents in the world.

On February 28, 1986 I married the love of my life, my soul mate, my best friend Russell Allan Spriggs. There could never be a more awesome, loving, understanding husband in the world. I love you so much, Russ.

More than words can say. I have been blessed with the two most wonderful, challenging, and fun sons in the world. Kenneth (Rich) Richmond, and Russell (Rusty) Spriggs. I love you! I have one grandson, who I love and worship, but I didn't get to see or spend quite enough time with or get to know. Carter, Grandma Toni will always love you.

Karen Gardner, my best bud and confidant, what would I have ever done without you the last 30+ years? Keep E.P. and J.D. in line. Yvette my dear friend, thank you for the gift of your friendship, and most of all thank you for letting me be

"Grammy" to my two very special Princess', Lauren and Tess, you'll never know how much I love all of you. Jolyn, Jill, Diane thanks for making work something more.

Dr. Ellington to you most of all... Thank you for the last 21+ years of my life you are truly a Saint. Thanks again everybody, see you on down the road. Please no flowers, no services, and no tears. Cremation by my request. A celebration of life to be announced. Arrangements entrusted to Deseret Memorial Mortuary. Condolences may be sent to the family at www.memorialutah.com."

❧

Gene Vincent

"#1 Rule: Dad Loves You! I want to first say, "goodbye" to my family, who I love very much. They are my whole life. I will miss fishing and hunting with them and my friends, but I will enjoy watching all of you do it from heaven. I love you all.

I am leaving behind to remember me, my loving wife, Brenda; my three children, Gene Jr., Mitch (Storee) and my beautiful daughter, Megan Joy; my grandkids, Cody, Twyla, Destiny; my mother, Beverly; my sister, Becky Robinson, my extended family and friends and my many pets.

I want to take care of Megan's college education, so in lieu of flowers please donate to the fund that has been set up at Credit Union One. I will haunt those of you that show up in a suit and tie – come casual."

❧

Laura Larsen Grames
"Sunshine"

"I was born August 18, 1969 in Salt Lake and died here too, on December 11, 2003. My dad (Kenneth Lloyd Larsen) and mom (Joyce Maurine Dickinson Larsen) are the two greatest parents anyone could want. I had a very happy childhood with my brother (Dale Larsen) and three sisters (Karen (Quo) Atwood, Brenda (Mark) Tilby, Regina (Allan) Fee). I've been blessed so much in my life and am so grateful. I love you all.

I met my best friend and soul mate, Steven Michael Grames and we were wed November 30, 1990. We were sealed for time and all eternity a year later. God let me struggle to get two precious boys, Ashlin and Murphy, so I would understand how special they are. I love my little family with all my heart. I'll always be here for you, forever.

I invented no miracle cures nor solved political crises. I simply was the best mom, wife, daughter, sister and friend I could be. Even at that, I fell short. Forgive me, please, if I hurt you. Love is so much easier to carry than hate. I may have suffered much through my life but it was so I could leave early and finish my work on the other side.

Remember – "You've got to keep breathing, 'cause tomorrow the sun will rise and who knows what the day will bring. In lieu of flowers, I request purple helium balloons to be released graveside."

Madeline C. Costanzo

"When tomorrow starts without me,
And I'm not there to see;
If the sun should rise and find your eyes
All filled with tears for me;
I wish so much you wouldn't cry
The way you did today,
While thinking of the many things
We did not get to say.
I know how much you love me,
As much as I love you,
And each time that you think of me,
I know you'll miss me too.
But when tomorrow starts without me,
Please try to understand,
That an angel came and called my name,
And took me by the hand,
And said my place was ready
In Heaven far above,

And that I'd have to leave behind
All those I dearly love.
But as I turned to walk away,
A tear fell from my eye,
For all my life I'd always thought,
I did not want to die.
I had so much to live for,
So much yet to do,
It seemed almost impossible,
That I was leaving you.
I thought of all the yesterdays,
The good ones and the bad,
I thought of all the love we shared,
And all the fun we had.
If I could relive my yesterday,
Just even for a while,
I'd say goodbye and kiss you
And maybe see you smile.
But then I fully realized,
That this could never be,
For emptiness and memories,
Would take the place of me,
And when I thought of worldly things,
I might miss come tomorrow,
I thought of you and when I did,
My heart was filled with sorrow.
But when I walked through heaven's gates
I felt so much at home.
When God looked down and smiled at me,
From His great golden throne,
He said, "This is eternity, and all I've promised you."
Today for life on earth has passed,
But here it starts anew.
I promise no tomorrow,
But today will always last.
And since each day's the same day,
There is no longing for the past.

But you have been so faithful,
So trusting and so true.
Though were times you did some things,
You knew you shouldn't do.
But remember I want to remind you,
You have always been forgiven.
And now at last you're free.
So won't you take me by the hand
And share my life with me?
So when tomorrow starts without me,
Don't think we're far apart,
For every time you think of me,
I'm right here, in your heart.
I will miss you all.
I loved you all I could.
Please be good to one another and be happy,
As you should.
I want to say goodbye right now
To all of you I've loved.
You have made my life a blessing
And taught me how to love.
For that, I thank you deeply.
And remember I am always near.
Goodbye.
For now, In passing I leave behind
My legacy of love,
My children – I Love them all
"As Big As The Sky!"

My daughter Kelli, her family, Marc, Nicole "Princess", Ryan, Brady, Jackson and Lucas. My son Scott, his family, Annette, Breanna, Emma "Lucia – My Heart" and Noah. My baby boy Kenny and his beautiful partner Alex. My children's father, Ken. My brother George, his wife Ann and his family. My best friend, Pammie (the sister I never had), her husband Allan and their family. My dear friend (big sister) Babs and her family."

For many individuals, the most important theme in their obituaries is surrounding their affiliation with churches, God and other spiritual philosophies.

Stella Langston

"To all my Family and Friends, this is the last written correspondence you will ever receive from me, because my Heavenly Father has called me to his side so I could share my love with all his children. I will be preparing Heaven for your return, making sure there is enough room for all of us to be together when we meet again. I want to take this time to thank everyone for making my life so full of love and happiness from its start to finish. When you think of me, please always remember how much I appreciated a reason to smile. It is my hope that our memories will be a reason to smile. I always loved life and I always loved you."

Vicky Burrows Williams
1946 - 2008

"I had an absolutely WONDERFUL LIFE! Thank you everyone that contributed to my happiness and loving care. I truly LOVED MY FATHER IN HEAVEN and I hope he will be tolerant of my imperfections and let me sneak in the back door of his kingdom where he lives.

I was born 23 February 1946 in Salt Lake City, Utah to my wonderful parents Chester Elmer Burrows & Ada R. Marshall Burrows. I met my beloved, precious, handsome, kind & thoughtful husband Richard Lee Williams when I was 16. We married two years later on Friday 13 March 1964. We were sealed nine months later by approval of the first Presidency of the LDS Church in the Salt Lake Temple, 16 December 1964.

Rick and I served in the Jordan River, St. George and Mt. Timpanogos Temples. I served in two Relief Society Presidencies and in many other callings. We had a wonderful life together. We traveled and played a lot. I am proud to say I am the great great granddaughter of President Wilford

Woodruff. We loved to do genealogy work for our families. I loved to read, I loved people and to keep journals.

I am survived by my precious husband, Rick, children, Wendy (Mike) Ipsen, Richard C. (Steph) Williams, David Rowdy (Lindsey) Williams and Stormy (Bryan) Goeckeritz, nine granddaughters and seven grandsons; mother, Ada Marshall Burrows and three sisters. My six-year-old daughter, Tammy Jo Williams and father, Chester E. Burrows, preceded me in death.

Two of my favorite sayings are "Put the shoe on the other foot and you will understand where they are coming from" and "We are not human beings having a spiritual experience, we are spiritual beings having a human experience.""

Lanny Pierce

"Hi guys! I know it's been a hard year... I've been watching. If you only knew how thin the veil is – all you need to do is LISTEN. Maybe you can't see me with your eyes, but I'm with each one of you. When you think of me, or ask for my help, I'm here. I wish you could feel the warm love where I am – It's incredible! I'm not only okay, I'm SUPER! I love you and all and I don't want you to see my absence as a death... actually it's more of a metamorphosis. Kinda like a caterpillar making the transformation into a butterfly, and Man can I fly! Please realize that this is your opportunity for growth – use me as a reason. And remember, prayers are like presents for me... they really help!"

AnnaLee Green Vallace

"I am writing to say thank you to all of those that impacted my life so greatly. I had wonderful parents, who taught me correct principles and raised me in the true gospel. I am very grateful for my membership in Christ's true church and the impact it has had on my life. Finally to all of the many wonderful people, and great beloved friends who have touched my heart and my life so tremendously. I have lived a very wonderful, joyful, full life. I hope that I have been able to share my happiness with others, and want my passing to be a time of happiness and celebration rather than a time of sorrow and grief. It is truly a time of joy, happiness, and celebration as I am now with those that I so dearly love and have missed. I have never wanted to be a burden upon anyone and do not want anyone to be burdened by my passing."

Ruth Olsen Pullan

"When you read this, I will be with my grandmother, mom, and son. I was born on December 15, the year is not important. My parents were Marinda and DeForest Olsen, they along with my two brothers "Fos" and Roy Olsen and my son Rod beat me home.

I will have left this world with a piece missing from my heart, perhaps that piece will be put back when I see my son once again. I am survived by my husband, Don "Let Me Tell You A Story" Pullan and my two daughters, Marla Ann (John Loomis) and Stephanie (Joe Leimkuhler). I must have done something right for the Lord to give me those two special spirits. (I am thankful my girls were here longer than I was). I am now on my knees telling the Lord how grateful I am for sending me, my two daughters, six grandchildren, two great-granddaughters, and my "Adopted" children John Henderson, and Susie Gale.

I was active in the LDS Church and served in many callings including President of the Relief Society and seven years with the Young Married Women. I worked many years, and made the decision that I could contribute more if I volunteered. I gave my time to many organizations and became President of most of them.

I organized the First Jail-A-Thon at the Crossroad Mall, raising the largest amount of money ever raised at that time for the Utah Cancer Society. One of my many loves was creating handmade quilts and braided rugs, of which I have won many awards including Grand Prize, and First Place at the State and County Fairs.

I love God, life, my family and my friends. I give thanks to the many people who have made my life a joy with their smiles and hugs, they know whom they are, and to my Bridge friends, do not grieve for me, as I will be waiting for you with the cards all dealt. I am taking the easy way out, so there won't be a viewing just a memorial, and in lieu of flowers take your loved ones out to dinner and tell them how special they are to you."

Young people whose lives had yet to be fully lived wrote some obituaries.

Carren T. Accord

"Hey Dad, I've come a calling. I've finished my short journey and now I'm home... we have so much catching up to do. I was a Mother's Day present, on May 20, 1954, to my parents Gina and Terry Twiller, who were residing in Provo, Utah. I lost you at the age of five as a result of an accident, and this reunion will be one of great joy to me. Grandma and I are a few checker games behind, so it's going to be a busy time. I had a wonderful life, which was made very special by my loving family.

There are so many things that I'll delight in remembering... my great attachments to God's special creatures: the magnificent cats. People were my delight and sometimes my downfall, but I have grown and learned from each encounter.

I really loved being "Aunt Carry" to my nieces and nephews. I'll miss the chance to take care of my plants, and appreciate all the beautiful things that abound in nature.

Mom, I know how much you loved me and I deeply regret the heartache that this must bring. You can chew me out later, OK?

We'll say our goodbyes on Tue. Sept. 4 at 2:30 PM. Peace and love – Till we meet again."

James Allen

"That's it. It's over. I've come a long way and here is where it ends. It's strange being dead. I'm sorry I went first, but it wasn't entirely up to me. I suppose it never really was. Some people said I was lucky, but I think it's more about how I looked at life. It's important not to let things get to you, nor take yourself too seriously."

I was born April 19th 1985. I was only 23, too young, I know. But I've learned a lot throughout my life, and along all my travels. Most importantly I learned the importance of relationships. I'm not just me. I'm a son, I'm a brother, a friend, a lover, and I'm a citizen, one part of a much larger whole. I'm an ally and an enemy, but more importantly I'm human. I may have learned this a bit too late in life, but nonetheless. So I leave now, countless relationships that defined who I was, and now being the ones to pass on my story they will forever continue to define who I am.

Well I sure as hell loved my life. I guess that's the point, isn't it? I'd like to hope there's more to it. I hope that, with all my efforts I was able to change something for the better. I hope that I was able to motivate others to grow and create growth around them.

Being that I never quite settled, I hope now that I've found my home. To ensure I have, please leave the casket and the black, ditch the viewing & funeral and join me April 19th 12 Noon for a celebration of my life. Bury my ashes and plant a tree, this will be my hope.

Fanantena

Espero

Espoir

Insallah

Hope"

Many obituaries address a worldview, which included travel, philosophy, education and associations with benevolent organizations.

Duffy" Casey

"Duffy left this final message for his friends and family: "I went Airborne today. What a fantastic journey through The Human Time Space Illusion. Some of it was magic and some of it tragic, but I had a good life all the way!

I had two of the greatest sons a father could know, Brandon and Oliver. My ex-wife (due to no fault of her own) Jo Anne Casey, Brandon's mother, is a saint and a fabulous Master of the Life Experience. Isabel Esparza (Casey), Oliver's mother is a beautiful soul who came into my life when I thought there wasn't much life left. God was I wrong! What a kick in the "duff" she has been.

To all my friends, I will miss you but I will see you again. A special thanks to my brother Joel for his constant support in my metaphysical and spiritual studies. I will see all of you again. Ditto.

My thanks, also, to all the fine people at the VA Hospital in Salt Lake City and Seattle. 'The day you were born you cried and the world rejoiced. Live your life so that the day you die the world cries and you rejoice. 'Namaste. PS: Oliver, be sure to mind your mother! I'll be checking in on you now and then."

It may be that I died every day of my life, regenerating in the process. To me, I walked in beauty; but, as with Flannery O'Connor's idea that beauty in the making is grotesque, things may have looked rather messy to others – and often so to myself.

Despite knowing what synergistic power woman and man together can create, I have lived many years without that alignment and raised six young children after the death of the marriage that bore them. My mother raised six children after my father's young death. We have had different trials, my mother and I, but have engaged in them with similar valiance. For over a decade, we restored antique lighting as Alfa Lite, Inc. business partners.

I have children and colleagues in India, China and Alaska – and also throughout the world as they have come to SLC and studied the ESL, philosophy, and communication I taught – whose names I may have forgotten but not my love for them. So also for those I coached in diving and water ballet, and those I taught at the University of Utah.

Other commitments include The Church of Jesus Christ of Latter-day Saints to which I am deeply indebted, The old, old Deseret Gym, The Broadway Stage, Utah Symphony Chorus, Salt Lake Opera Company, The University of Utah Departments of Communication, and of Nutrition; Retrenchment friends, Bells and Bowls musicians, Sufism, friend Touraj, dear ones I attended through hospice work, culinary arts, and bicycling.

The children of my womb honor me in the refinement of their character, the growth in their marriages and children; also in their creativity and especially in their love for each other, the Lord, the earth, and all humanity – living, future and dead. I go to prepare a feast like we never held, in the courtyards we've yet to realize, with company, repartee, and joy we seldom knew to dream for.

Humor, Friendship, Surrender, Forgiveness, Imagination, and especially Spirit carried me when I sagged. Through death, will I yet "wake up young from this trance" of mortality.

When young I was fascinated by references in scripture to "divers places." I initially interpreted that to mean under water and in the sky, but hope it to mean 'something unlike anything else.' To enter such realms I go from you physically, to yet meet anon."

❧

Vicki Gillespie Mickelsen
1944 - 2006

"For the genealogists: Born, July 23, 1944 Wichita, Kansas. Parents: Col. Victor A. Gillespie and Lois May (Peggy) Wright Gillespie. Brothers: James Marshall and William Bruce. Degrees: Indianola High School 1962; BA University of Kansas 1966 Spanish and French; MA Indiana University 1968 Spanish; PhD Indiana University 1974 Spanish; MA University of Utah 1983 Linguistics. Married: David Jeffrey Mickelsen (1967-2003). Daughters: Anna Grace and Kristina Elisabeth. Died: September 22, 2006 from a fourth and final encounter with cancer.

For the world: As a last word, I want to share what I have found most wonderful about this life I am ending. First of all is the miracle of my beautiful, talented, and loving daughters, who have filled my life with joy and pride since the moment I first held them. Nurturing them and watching them develop into the lovely women they have become has been the best adventure of my life. An adventure shared with my life's companion David, who not only sheltered and cared for me at home but also took me journeying around the world, enriching my life in often-unexpected ways.

Next are the many friends with whom I have shared joys and sorrows, trivia and crises, food and fun. I have been blessed throughout my life with the companionship of compatible souls, and I hope I have contributed equally to their wellbeing. The love and support of my friends has been incredibly sustaining during this final illness and I thank them with every breath.

Apart from people, I have loved and engaged in many activities. First of all is music. Over the last 30 years, I have been privileged to belong to the Ad Hoc Singers, the Salt Lake Vocal Ensemble, and most recently, Jubilate.

My second great love has been houses, especially historic houses. This enthusiasm has guided our steps as tourists (never met a castle I didn't like) and our choice of residence (beautiful Victorian on the National Register). It also led me into community service, including the establishment of the University Historic District in 1991 and six years as a member of the Historic Landmark Commission for Salt Lake City.

Another guiding enthusiasm has been the Spanish language and Hispanic culture, with which I fell in love at age 13. This love guided my choice of academic specialty and led me to work for many years at the Guadalupe Center and Guadalupe School, and then to teach Spanish at the University of Utah.

Finally, I want to mention my home away from home, 3M Health Information Systems, whose excellent software I have lovingly and patiently documented for the past 20 years, in the company of wonderful coworkers whose talent and sense of humor have made working for a living into a truly enjoyable and soul- satisfying experience. Another way my life has been truly blessed.

When I was a student in Latin America, I discovered the following poem, which has guided my thinking about life and death and which I pass on to all who read this: Must I then go alone? Will nothing of me remain in this world? At least songs. At least flowers. A memorial celebration will be held.

HEY… those better not be tears I see or sobs I hear. I have had such a wonderful life I don't regret any minute of it. Thank you everyone."

R. Paul Cracroft

"Ironic, huh? First time my pic's run in the paper in years, and I'm not around to clip the obit. Tough! I was called up by heart trouble, cancer, diabetes, etc… elderly man stuff. But few have had a more delightful time on Earth than I and you can bet your last buck I'd have hung around, given a choice.

I decided at age 13 that I wanted to write. At 16 I was elected editor of East High's Red & Black for 1939 and won the first All-American rating for a high school paper in Utah's history.

After working for a year to save the exorbitant tuition costs at the University of Utah ($30 per quarter during the Depression!), I enrolled there, majoring in English and writing for all of the student publications, winning campus and regional honors and editing the literary magazine, Pen, in 1948.

My friend Heber Hart arranged a fateful blind date for me on Aug. 23, 1941, with Kathryn Storrs. She and I celebrated our 63rd wedding anniversary in 2007.

From June 1942 to July 1944, I served in the North Central States mission, headquartered in Minneapolis. If the field was white and ready to harvest, I must have served out-of-season, but I enjoyed my 25 months away from my lady-in-waiting, making few converts beside myself.

When I returned home in late July 1944, the draft board all but met my bus. Kay and I were married in the Salt Lake Temple by Elder (later President) Harold B. Lee on Aug. 16, 1944. Then I donned the uniform of a buck private at Ft. Douglas to train at Camp Roberts, CA. Kay went with me.

When the Battle of the Bulge hit at Christmastime 1944, I was sent to Ft. Benning, GA, where I was commissioned a shavetail lieutenant. I shipped out on Aug. 12, 1945, on the USS George Clymer for what I later learned was the planned invasion of Japan. Messrs. Tojo and Hirohito had learned I was coming, so in wise terror, they surrendered when I was just two days at sea.

Re-entering college in January 1947 (BA '48, MA '54), I worked as a reporter for The Salt Lake Tribune and then for Parry Sorensen as assistant director of public relations at the "U." From 1951 to 1955, I served in Washington, D.C., as first press secretary to the late Senator Wallace F. Bennett.

Returning to the "U" in 1955, I worked for more than 35 years in public relations as executive director of the Alumni Association, director of Lectures and Concerts, instructor in Journalism and, until my retirement in 1990, as manager of Kingsbury Hall. In this last position I initiated the first serious considerations that led to renovation of that great hall.

From 1959-1973, I hosted "Retrospect," a news analysis show on KUED, Channel 7, which, in those early years, made it the longest-running sustained weekly program on the educational channel. Walter Cronkite I was not, but then he was no Paul Cracroft!

For 36 years I also served as statistician for the U's home football games, typing play-by-plays and spotting for Paul James at "away" games during many of those years.

As an active member of the LDS Church, I have been blessed to serve twice as a member of the High Council of the University of Utah Stake, twice as a bishopric counselor, Bishop of the Parleys Fourth Ward (1977-1982), and Parleys Stake high councilman.

I helped write the History of Parleys Stake from its official founding in 1958 to 2000. I have been an officer or teacher in all Church auxiliaries since I was 16.

For four years, I was primary caregiver to my sweet Kay during her onset of Alzheimer's disease until September 2004, when I underwent surprise surgery for a malignant thymus coupled with six- bypass heart surgery. There followed five weeks of radiation and months of rehab to learn how to walk and regain balance and how to talk and swallow again, thanks to a paralyzed vocal cord. My scratchy voice led me to rename myself "Golden Throat."

Wherever life has taken me, I've kept writing. In 1979 I published A Certain Testimony, a 479-page epic poem based on the Book of Mormon. I have written several plays. Sam's Place dealt with the history of Sam Weller's Zion Book Store and was staged by both City Rep and the Babcock Performing Readers at the "U." Later the BPR staged Letter Perfect, a mixture of fact and fiction told through a long exchange of letters. Officer's Mess dealt with a personal experience during the occupation of Japan. Another play, Escape to Freedom, tells the true story of feisty Liuda Avizonis, who led her family out of Lithuania when she was just six years old, past Russian and German soldiers. In the days just before my death, I was putting the finishing touches on yet another play, Shadows on the Moon, based on the scriptural account of Coriantumr.

I fully expect that I am now reunited with my sweetheart Kay, who passed away in September 2007, and with grandsons Thomas Paul and Bryant Jeffrey Parker, who left us early to gather bricks for our mansion in heaven. Immediate family who also did not "go gentle into that good night" were my parents and older brother Laurance White Cracroft. I hope to see the rest of you later!"

R. Davis Bitton

"I, Ronald Davis Bitton, have moved on to the next stage of existence. As you read this, I am having a ball rejoining my parents and grandparents, uncles, aunts, cousins, and dear friends and associates I knew on earth.

I am wide awake, no longer struggling with the narcolepsy that handicapped but did not defeat me, and cheerfully taking in the new state of affairs and accepting the callings that will occupy me there.

It has been an abundant life. Growing up in Blackfoot, Idaho, where I was born on 22 February 1930, and on a farm in nearby Groveland, I never felt one moment of familial insecurity. My parents, Ronald Wayne and Lola Davis Bitton, loved me and did everything they could to see that I had opportunities, including piano lessons from age six. I learned to work in the house, in the yard, on the farm, and in local retail stores. I learned to write as a reporter for the Daily Bulletin. I remember enjoying a trip to the San Francisco world's fair, fishing and hunting trips, scouting camps, and community concerts.

I had great friends and was elected to several student offices. I learned to compete in softball and basketball. I joined a crack high school debating team. As a student at Brigham Young University, missionary in France, enlisted man in the U.S. Army, and graduate student at Princeton University, I felt myself growing in understanding. I went on to be a professor of history at the University of Texas at Austin, the University of California at Santa Barbara, and for 29 years the University of Utah, enjoying many congenial students and colleagues.

I have presented papers at scholarly conventions and published articles and books. I have loved good food, good books, the out of doors, music, art, the dappled things. A nurturing home throughout my life has been the Church of Jesus Christ of Latter-day Saints. Bishops, stake presidents, teachers, mission presidents, and general authorities I have known people I could admire and follow. My own opportunities to serve have been numerous, starting at a very young age and including elder's quorum president, counselor in a bishopric, member of the stake high council, and gospel doctrine teacher for many years. From 1972 to 1982 I served as assistant church historian. I have loved the hymns, the scriptures, and the temple.

I am grateful for Aunt Vilate Thiele, my mother's sister, a steady friend; my other uncles and aunts on both sides; my brother John Boyd Bitton; my sisters Marilyn Bitton Lambson and Elaine Bitton Benson; wonderful nephews and nieces; children Ronald Bitton, Kelly Bitton Burdge, Timothy Bitton, Jill Cochran, Stephanie Ross, Debbie Callahan, Larry Morris, Judy Nauta, Earl Morris, Delbert Morris; their spouses; and 56 grandchildren and great-grandchildren, all of whom are to me a delight. Having learned the value of loyalty, I appreciated the affection and interest of my family as well as cherished friends.

No one has been more important to me than my dear wife and companion JoAnn, a woman loved by all who knew her. She rallied to my side, stood by me through thick and thin, grew with me, laughed with me, made good things happen, and, marvel of marvels, agreed to be my companion through time and all eternity. I have not lived a perfect life, but I have tried. And I know in whom I have trusted."

Lena Cook "Lee"

"Please do not mourn my passing on as I have had a truly happy and wonderful life. I was born into the happy and loving family of Bill and Carmel Cribari, as the younger sister of Carl and the older sister to George, who was born four years later. I was raised and schooled in Denver where I met and married my high school sweetheart Ray Cook after he served four years in the Navy during World War II. He was my perfect mate and a doting father to our three sons, Daniel (deceased) (Rhea Paige Cook), Thomas and David.

After retiring Ray and I spent much of our time traveling in and out of the country and it was such great fun. Being a housewife, homemaker, mother and grandmother, plus volunteering were most on my mind.

I was a dedicated member of The Assistance League, Newcomers Club, P.E.O. Chapter "N" Judge Memorial Boosters, St. Mary's Guild, St Ambrose Altar Society as secretary and treasurer. I was also involved in St. Vincent de Paul as hospitality and reservation committee chairman, Catholic Ladies League, Catholic Ladies Bowling League and Saturday night Dinner- Dance Club.

Survived by husband Ray of 60+ years; brothers Carl Cribari and George (Cis) Cribari; sons Thomas (Susan), David (Heather); grandchildren Aimee O'Brien (Tom), Corrine Cook Fond (Greg), Lindsey Luttmer (Dallas), Jennifer, Perri and Devin; also great-grandchildren Megan, Jon Jon and Katie O'Brien and many loving nieces, nephews and cousins in Denver.

To my wonderful friends, my sincere thanks for the many kindnesses shown to me during my recent illness. The beautiful flowers sent to me, the cards, the phone calls as well as your personal visits and your prayers and good wishes were so appreciated. So till we meet again, know that I love you all!"

❧

Vicki Lou Peterson Harker
"Everything is Temporary"

"I passed away peacefully on March 14, 2009 surrounded by her loving family. I was born to Lucille and Kenneth Peterson. My father was in the military so I enjoyed travel and living in California, Alabama, Texas, Michigan, Japan, New Jersey and Utah. I graduated from Provo High School in 1957.

After attending the University of Utah for a short time, I met my true love. I was totally smitten with Melvyn Harker, whom I married in 1959. We are the proud parents of Brad, Melani (Chandra) and Marie (Jim). We were later divorced and remained friends. I am delightfully survived by three beautiful grandchildren: Katlin, Jessica and Will. My mother, father and my brother, Karl, preceded me in death.

I worked at Planned Parenthood Association of Utah for six years. I resumed my studies at the University of Utah graduating with a B.S. in Sociology, specializing in Criminology and Corrections. I retired from the Utah State Department of Corrections October 2001 after 20 years of service."

Bevan Chipman

"My journey began December 30, 1934. The ultimate journey started on September 8, 2007. I have always been fond of calling Magna my "home town". I particularly enjoyed and appreciated the different ethnic and social mix of people and friends. A couple of friends and I sailed from Sydney, around Australia, through the Indian Ocean and the Suez Canal. We traveled through Western Europe and crossed the Atlantic on the "original" Queen Mary.

Having my summers free I started traveling to Spain and Mexico, sketching, painting, and studying the language. I finally made it back to Italy (five trips) to learn Italian and to paint. During this time I was actively involved with the Utah Watercolor Society, the Utah Arts Council and spent 20-plus years working with the Ririe-Woodbury Dance Company on their advisory board. These were rich and rewarding times and I so enjoyed my association with Shirley and Joanne and the dancers. It's been good. Ciao."

These obituaries were written by people who do not have a specific date with death, but who wrote their last words "just in case". At some point they will join the others in their own specific categories.

Kevin Harding

"Mining and working as a diesel mechanic have been my lifetime vocations. I would not recommend that anyone choose the first since I almost lost my life (much too soon), twice. I was lucky to come away with only one missing ear."

Kenneth Robert Bertran

"I had one last bike ride and although I go on alone, don't grieve for my passing. Instead, rejoice in the beauty of our magnificent world and follow your heart to each new adventure. I leave my wife, Eve, who is my partner and my love, for a short time only until we can be reunited again for more wonderful adventures together. We shared a love of adventure to different areas of the world riding on two wheels either motorcycle or bicycles.

Enjoy each day you have during your time here and enjoy your family and friends. I will miss my son Chris, my daughters Laura and Libby and their partners Valerie, Carl and Chad.

If I leave with regret it is only because I wanted to teach my granddaughters Ireland and Isabelle how to ride a bike and enjoy riding with them.

In life don't cry because it's over, smile because it happened."

Don Wingeleth

"I was born at home in Cleveland, Ohio and was raised by my mom. If I must say, she did a good job. After high school, I worked for a few years and was drafted into the Korean War. I came home and with the aid of the GI Bill and $551.20 that I won in the Daily Double at Thistledown Racetrack, I went to OSU. (Most of you around here think that I'm referring to Oregon or Oklahoma State, but I'm talking about Ohio State University.) A couple of weeks after graduation, I met a gorgeous redhead named Sallie... and that's when my life began, though I didn't know it at the time. Four months later we got married and had six terrific kids. When they grew up and left home, we looked back and I realized what a truly wonderful life I'd had. That's hard to beat. Well, for now, I'll let you guys go. I want to thank all of my friends that I've met over the years including those at the Hidden Valley Country Club. You and my family meant the world to me. As they say in the "industry"... "Take Five".

Fred Young

"Music has always been a part of my life, since my father won a piano and I started music lessons. I taught 400 students and I thoroughly enjoyed every one of them, even those who didn't practice."

Carol Mitchell
"Big Heart"

"I have only slipped away into the next room. I am I, and you are you. Whatever we were to each other that we still are. Call me by my old familiar name, speak to me in the easy way you always used to. Wear no forced air of solemnity or sorrow. Laugh at the little jokes we enjoyed together. Play, smile, think of me, and pray for me.

Let my name be ever the household word that it always was. Let it be spoken without the ghost of a shadow on it. Life means all that it ever meant… there is absolutely unbroken continuity. I am waiting for you – somewhere near, just around the corner of the river. All is well."

Dr. Charles E. Edwards

"I guess it was time for me to depart from my earthly sojourn. It has been a fabulous trip. I have loved and been loved by my wonderful family. The choice people I have met along the way have brought me much joy and satisfaction. Thanks to all who have made my life so great. See you all again, but you needn't hurry for my sake. I will be patiently waiting."

Mark Silverman

"My name is Mark Silverman. Sooner or later I'll be leaving this existence. I don't know exactly when so I'm writing this now. I want my life to have counted for something. My concept of this may change, but so far I have learned that the older

I get the more experience I gain and the easier life gets. Also that life passes by quickly, so enjoy it! Keep a good sense of humor. I'd like others to understand how to be better people, or be the best they can be. One of the most important things we can have is compassion for our fellow beings. High on the list of things that made me happy was the meeting of my wife Nancy. One of the unhappiest occurrences was the death of Mr. Al Ziegler. All I ask is that my funeral is honest and sincere. Mark"

Here is a special lady. She was an important member of my hospice graduating class. This perfectly describes her. Every time I read her words, I burst into a smile.

Nichole Hoecher Thompson

"Nichole Hoecher Thompson died of mortality today. It wasn't the pound of provolone cheese a day, or more dark chocolate than "real food", I still only had a cholesterol count of 107, truly the envy of all who knew my eating habits. I maintained a strict 100 fat gram a day diet, but in the end it was death that killed me.

I am survived by all the lucky S.O.B.'s still living, as well as my husband Dominic, (a truly patient man) two wonderful boys: Dallas and Zachary. They will miss their mother terribly, but bid adieu cheerfully to those "Prozac moments". Dallas once said (at age 7): "PMS is when ladies can't answer simple questions peacefully". Well mom's about as peaceful as she's gonna get now.

I will be cremated and the remains stored in a small barrel around my husband's neck, just in case he might forget me. At least he has those subliminal weight loss tapes to laugh about.

I was a humanitarian to the end and held an abundance of compassion in my heart. I was very fond of good movies, The Simpsons and Brad Pitt, and I never, not once, ever had penis envy. I loved life and will miss it."

Teddy Armstead

"Well I guess this is it! I hope they give me time to stop and talk to Mom, Dad and Bob. I had a good time growing up. I made a good choice in picking Mary for my partner. We had great kids.

Have fun and be careful. I have gone home."

Neil Grant

"This supremely conscious observer that I now recognize as my soul, this marble of essence that is who and what I am, that cannot die is reclaimed to the universe. See you in the future, dear and delightful brother. It feels so good out I think I'll leave it out!"

Jackie Lynn

"Well, if you are reading this, I was just dying to get here! Ha! Ha! Oh what a life I've had. Many adventures some good, some bad, some not worth remembering but they happened. I lived well, loved much and laughed often. Cried some, fought some, I could go on and on. Thank You Tina at GYN Affiliates you're the best!"

A celebration of her life will be held at the The Woods on Ninth."

Carl Nester

"I died at my home in the mountains I came to love in Park City. I loved my beautiful wife, and the three children she bore me. I had many vocations and hobbies and I enjoyed them all. I was most proud of my high school and college years, karate, and teaching school and my jobs as a policeman, firefighter and lifeguard. I loved the feeling of saving lives and helping people. My life was as full as a man's could be and I leave this earth without regrets other than its shortness."

Marlon Brown

"Goodbye, my friends. It's hard to die when all the birds are singing in the sky. Now that spring is everywhere – think of me and I'll be there."

Karren Shred

"As my life ends I shall always cherish the things you have shared and given me: a better understanding of people, the world, and what my place has been in it. Your wisdom, patience and laughter have made my life easier and hard times a lighter burden to bear."

Cynthia Ellen Dennis

"I came here, knowing all that lied ahead. Thinking all of the time, what an adventure this life is! Knowing that I am loved oh-so-much and giving in return. Life. Oh beautiful life... so simple, yet so... complex. I came; I've grown, lived and loved. Now, it's time to gather my knowledge and experiences; give you my memories of what once was and what may be again; into my basket of life for my return back to where I came. To live – to love will never be lost my friend. I will always dwell in your heart as you do in mine.

I was a caring and giving spirit, willing to go to any length to make sure someone was taken care of. I loved the challenge of bringing out the success in people. If friends were in need, I would offer counsel to help them resolve whatever issues they were facing. It was in my nature to love and protect anyone. I would like to be best remembered for my ability to gain new friendships with anyone."

Hank Samson

"If you are reading this, then I'm dead. I will finally, maybe, have the answer to the riddle of life. If I do, I'll try to give you a hint. Stop for a moment and listen very carefully. If you don't hear anything that means that dying has been no help at all.

I wrote this in preparation because I didn't know when I would die. Whenever it was, it was too damn soon. I didn't want to leave the people I love, especially my beautiful (inside and out) and difficult wife, Noreen; and my wonderful and terrible children, Sarah, Molly and Liam. Thank you for being in my life, for making the trip so much richer.

Thanks to all my other teachers, also: my parents, my brother and sisters, and my great friends. Thanks to Demeter for beer; and to the poets, for the words; and to J.D., for reminding me of what they mean; and to Craig, for making me write this."

※

Happily, this guy isn't dead yet. Remember Scrooge? There may still be hope for change. The writing of your obituary might bring a "wake-up" call. It is curious that he wrote about himself in the third person. I think saying these words in first person might have been too disquieting.

T.L. Zweilig

"Today died one of the most selfish, arrogant, ungrateful, self-pitying, mean, vicious, castigating, ruthlessly devaluing, vain, moody, irritable, rage-filled and hostile sons-of-bitches that ever bragged his life was worthless. He used people for what he could get, manipulating them, prostituting himself for what little affection his recalcitrant stone heart would let him see.

There was never any shortage of other people around him in his life, all eager to offer love, but when it came to love, he was a blind, deaf, paralyzed, insensate mute. Only his bumptious whining, his garish hauteur and his generalized scornful disdain matched his limitless self-loathing and endless self-hatred for others.

He fooled some. He was bright enough to use "fancy language to cover deception, but never talk about real feeling" – that was how the last of the string of women he used described it. His lovers, his so-called "intimate partners," were women he loved to hate.

He had good, honest friends. One said he was "a lot of work."

Another was bold enough to say, "You make me nervous." Still another pointed out his pattern of being drawn to empty women, always hoping to find something in them that he should have been looking for within himself, but then, what else might you expect from one who was "more alienated from (his) family than anyone else I've ever known."

With him gone, the living will suffer less, and a little less love will be sucked irretrievably into an identity-less black hole of selfishness. With that, there may be a modicum of relief for those who survive him.

As for him, he long envied the dead while living, so perhaps the rancid ache of his pervasive, fetid greed now knows relief as well."

❧

The following are obituaries written by those who have battled injuries, diseases or illness. These obituaries differ in tone and content than the others. There is a clarity to these obituaries that you do not find with others that have the time to change them over the years.

Joyce Bronson

"I was born Nov. 15, 1928 to two wonderful parents, Mary Smith and Parley Dunn. I am the younger sister of Al (his wife Mary). I graduated from North High and later continued my education at the University of Ohio. During my 20th year I met the love of my life, Tom Bronson. I was blessed with two loving children Gill and Joan (husband Ted). My husband enjoyed success in the insurance industry and together we provided a loving and spiritual home for our family. My children gave me three beautiful grandchildren that I love with all my heart. In 1990 I was diagnosed with cancer. I waged a courageous battle but on Dec. 4 1991 surrounded by my loving family I was released from my affliction. Many individuals helped me in my fight and I thank them all. Now I am gone but will watch over and take care of you as I have in the past. Thank God for family, friends and the love that will last."

Bess Seldon Marsden

"I was brought into this world in Vancouver, Washington by the greatest and most loving parents, Miles and Mary Seldon. My existence in this world ended on June 1, 1989, after a year-long battle with cancer. A graduate of Crescent High in '67 and pursued a career in sales; most recently with Cary's Accounting Svc.

I wait for my adorable husband of 14 years Chuck Marsden. We have grown and shared so many happy times on our boat at Clear Lake. I leave behind my mother and father, of Seattle, two caring and understanding brothers, and their families. I take with me the memories of a very close extended family and of many dear friends and acquaintances. I request that donations be made to the Ronald McDonald House."

Hammond Keogh

"Today I pass from this earth at home without the aid of my Rand McNally road map. After a second battle with cancer, I chose a quality of life taking time to see my friends and family over useless medical procedures. In remembrance of me and in lieu of flowers, my wish is for you to visit a scenic place of value and read one historical marker for me.

Life is for living! Make every day a holiday!"

Mel Harder

"Since I have been unable to fully communicate with family and friends for the past few years, I am relying upon my loved ones left behind to express a few thoughts on my passing. I have now joined my beloved wife Sharon in our new realm and assignment. The things I cherish most:

1. My family, both those I am now with and those left behind.

2. I am pleased to be a Wyoming native, and have graduated from Utah State and to have been able to serve my country in a career with the BLM.

3. I was pleased to be of service to the Lord."

❧

Yale Thomason

"If you are reading this obit.... well, I made it this long. I was hoping for a bit more, because I had things to do, places to go, people to meet. The first few years I have been bound and gagged in a chair with ALS. Complications resulting from the disease finally sent me to see St. Peter. Life has been good to me. I married Sharon Smith, a high school classmate and sweetheart. It might be a little presumptuous for me to be writing this, but sometime ago the doc said I had this long to live, so get your life in order. I don't particularly like the word "funeral" until you break it down from the root words: FUN – FER – ALL. So instead you are invited to a "celebration wake". My long-term address will be Plat x Salt Lake City Cemetery.

Some highlights are:
Romping around through East Millcreek as a child.
Working for Mr. Sears and Roebuck for 15 years
Owning AAA installers (Our motto: Plumb, Level and Square)
Member Utah Orchid Society (everyone should grow an orchid sometime)
To be born, I have to die from life as I know it."

❧

Ashley Nicole Bartos

"I wanted to live – I wanted to dance at my wedding with my loving fiancé Cody, and plan a life together. But cancer cut those dreams short. After three and a half years of pain and almost two years of treatments, my body finally wore out no matter how strong my spirit."

Her family added the following: "She was full of joy and danced and sang through her short life. Her quirky sense of humor brought laughter to many and we're sure she's teaching her famous "Spastic Dance" to the angels. Ashley loved fashion and never met a pair of shoes or a lip gloss she didn't like. She was an expert at hair and makeup and loved to give her friends makeovers. The strength and grace she demonstrated during her illness endeared her to her caregivers and were a source of inspiration to all of us. Please don't wear mourning clothes. Ashley loved bright colors and would want you to share happy memories of her."

Alice Kaye Lunnen Lippmann
"Grandma K"

"I lost my life to seven years of cancer treatment and a stroke. I was married at age twenty- one and a half to Kenneth Arthur Lippmann and from that marriage a daughter was born, Kristy Kaye. She and her husband Brian gave birth to four wonderful grandchildren, which have all been the light of my life. Over the years we've had lots of adventures to remember.

The most important thing I've learned is to spend the maximum amount of time with those you truly care for, that way when you get to the point in your life where I am you won't have any regrets. Please remember me the way I was."

This one is special. Bill was my good friend and allowed me to be part of his obituary. In the end, the calories coming in didn't equal those going out (he was a Dr.). He realized he had limited calories left. Willie thanks for spending those precious calories on this.

Dr. William M. Green

"Dear family and friends, I have begun a new journey today, a journey that all of us will eventually have to embark upon. I had been blessed with good health for most of my life; for which I was grateful, but for the last several months, the quality of my life was in a steady decline. I am happy now to begin my next journey. Like many other people I had many hobbies I enjoyed. The golf games, the fishing trips, the time spent at Flaming Gorge, all of these times have special and fond memories for me. I cannot help but feel that the true measure of a person's life is his relationship with the people he comes in contact with. Over the past several months, the outpour of concern and love from family and friends (I consider my patients as friends) has been overwhelming. The physical and emotional drain was tremendous, which made it impossible for me to respond to each and every person, please forgive me. If the caring and love, which has been shown to me, is any indication of a man's life, mine was not wasted. I would like to give a very special thank you to my wife Maggie. Her rock solid support and love was a major help to my physical and mental well-being during these times. Thank you honey. I'm ready now; it's time for me to say goodbye."

About a month after Bill died, I was playing golf alone on one of our favorite courses. The last hole of the day runs along a river. As I walked, I noticed a whirlwind in the center of the fairway. It appeared to be moving toward me. I attempted to avoid it by walking more to the river, but it seemed to follow me. As I reached the river's edge it engulfed me. Leaves, dust, wind, swirling around me for what seemed like a long time. I remember feeling embraced and immobile. It left me with peaceful chills and moved to my right, over the center of the slow moving river. Amazingly, it just stopped and the leaves gently drifted down to the water. I followed them as far as I could, and said "Goodbye for now, Willie, thanks for the good times. I know you'll always be with me in the wind".

LuAnn Lopez Vogt
"Forever in Our Hearts"

"Today, I took my last breath. It was a four-year battle with ovarian cancer that I thought I had won. I have to believe there is a reason why this happened. I would love to be able to understand why I'll never be able to jump on the back of my Cliff's (husband) motorcycle and ride just to ride.

I loved my life I had so many beautiful friends. I have found peace in my life and love that my heart hurts just thinking about it. I have been one of those lucky people that were able to laugh out loud and cry until I thought I could almost feel my heart break.

Living life to its fullest is something I have always tried to do. I have taught my three children to laugh each day, to smell the sunshine and to believe in the goodness of people. The hardest part of leaving is saying goodbye to my children. When you see them please remind them how much I love them. I also leave a wonderful husband Cliff. He has made my life what it is today. Cliff, keep your hands in the ride at all times. Having fun has always been his motto.

As I leave my loved ones behind, the ones that I lost will welcome me. I am preceded in death by my baby brother, Frankie and in the last two years my family has felt much heartache with the passing of my brother John and then watching my mom, Onnie Lopez pass away from a broken heart. I also leave behind my many friends I have met throughout my life. I never missed an opportunity to meet new people."

Tim Murphy
"Husband, Dad and Grandpa"

"Dear Family and Friends: I finally received my mission call March 22. 2003 You are all invited to the farewell being held March 27th. While living on this earth for the past 48 years I have had some great experiences. The best joys in my life have been knowing and loving my children. Oh how I will miss those tender loves!

I gave my Mom and Dad, a run for their money, but am grateful they raised me in the Church. I love the Savior, and the Gospel. Being sealed for time and eternity to my best friend and sweetie, Diane has been the best thing that has ever happened till now.

I have been ready for their "call" for some time. You all know I fought to stay here for you as long as I could. I promise to be close to you now and always. Goodbye to BYU Football, Utah Jazz, and antique cars. I won't miss hospitals, chemo, pain, sleepless nights, cold weather, or bills.

Love to you, Tim, Mary Kay Robison. If you are reading this, I must have closed my eyes for the last time and begun a new journey of joy and love without physical pain. I have concluded a 22 month battle with cancer, an awful disease which robs you of the precious energy and strength needed to live life to its fullest.

I can say that my life has been a wonderful journey, even though it hasn't always turned out as I had envisioned. It's been filled with joy, love and beauty, balanced at times by the difficult lessons life teaches.

I shared the last years of my life with my sweetheart, husband and partner, Kenny Ray Robison. I couldn't have asked for a more cherished lover, friend and companion with whom to share my life. More importantly, I couldn't have found a more loving man to be the father of our children, nor a better partner to help me make my final transition. Ken, your gentle and compassionate care made my illness bearable. I hope all the men reading this take note of how much strength it truly takes to show such caring and compassion. We had such fun together, sweetheart. Go now, and have some fun without any more lists or chores. You deserve to play! I ask those of you that love and care for Ken to love him now, and help him to move on without me.

My family made my passing a moment of joy and peace. One of life's most important lessons is that of showing our family and friends love while they are living. So, in this respect, I am requesting no flowers for me. Instead, please express your feelings of love and affection by making a donation to Huntsman Cancer Institute, whose doctors and staff I cannot thank enough for giving me extra time to spend with my loved ones. Better yet, take your spouse or family to lunch and tell them you love them today, for no one knows what tomorrow holds. I'm on to a new journey now, so wish me God's speed. I'm dancing with the angels now!"

Oliver Winn

"My picture on this page means that I have finally died. After at least one previous brush with the Grim Reaper. AIDS did the trick, as I have always known it would. This was no "valiant battle" I hated the whole thing. Much gratitude to Dr Excell and Maggie. They are smart, competent and caring. If you have to do the AIDS thing, you want to do it with these two. If I could afford it I would name you all. I hope that I have done a decent job in conveying how I have liked and loved you for your friendship and support through my difficulties without seeing it in print. Please skip the flowers, lovely as they are, in a few days they will be as dead as I am. Instead, send some $ to the Utah AIDS Foundation."

Beverly (Bev) David

"How Far Is Heaven? I hate to travel... so if heaven was too far, I went shopping instead. After more than two years trying. I found that even non-smokers have a hard time beating lung cancer. I worked for more than 37 years in banking operations. I loved to work because I was always blessed to work with "great friends" not just business associates. My final weeks were improved by the care I received from IHC Hospice team members."

Rae Thompson

"My Sweet Angel, I asked for a little longer – Death managed a smile. "You're right," I conceded; "How could I have been so foolish?" Cancer finally got me – got me good. But only my body. Turns out that Plato was right; the soul is immortal! Death has no sting, but it did create a change of address.

A few final thoughts, if I may: Cory, my love for you is eternal – you will forever be an inextricable part of my soul. Boys, how much I love each of you and appreciated being your Mother. Help Dad in the kitchen, and don't forget to change your socks! To extended family and friends: Thanks for your love and friendship; it's been a wonderful journey.

And by the way, Dad; Mom is more beautiful than ever!"

Bob Reiser
"Loving Husband, Dad, Brother, Cousin, and Friend"

"I passed away peacefully in my sleep after a six-year battle with cancer. I was born to Marjorie Chipman and Henry Wallace Reiser in Salt Lake City, Utah. Evidently, I told jokes the whole way out of the womb. I was infamous for setting back the clock on my sister Tanny's back–tickling sessions and sneaking the car with my cousin Margie Ann.

At the age of nine, I met the love of my life – a sexy, young pixie of three years – while I was running over her with my bicycle. I broke her leg. She broke my arm. The rest was fate, and I married her, JoAnn Seegmiller, on November 18, 1960. We were happily married for 43 years and sired two absolutely perfect children.

I was also a dedicated servant to this country's armed forces. I saw active duty at Fort Ord, California, during the Korean War where my buddies, my jeep, a lake, and I were casualties of the malted beverages served at the NCO club. A force of nature on the golf course, I was never earlier than five minutes late to a tee time. My growl after applying the 195-yard 8-iron into the trees at Forest Dale became legendary as it was retold during lunch at the Cotton Bottom. I was also pivotal in organizing the Annual Golf Banquet until my son, Papoose, and brother-in-law, Lincoln, assumed these executive duties.

I was a passionate advocate of wine tastings and worked tirelessly to sample all the great Zinfandels available in Zion. My close friends, Renz and the Little Giant, were integral in helping me with this important cause. My other great purpose in life was bestowing nicknames upon everyone with great affection. I attended East High School and the University of Utah."

※

Becke Jean Probert
"Sister, Daughter, Teacher, Friend"

"I was born April 15, 1960; I succumbed to my battle of cervical cancer in the early morning of November 7, 2009, within two months of diagnosis. My family stayed with me during this time and they wished me a peaceful journey to the next life. During this time, I was able to have many wonderful visits with my family and friends, who were supportive of me. We were the "Probert" girls. We spent many vacations, dinners, Shakespearean Festivals, laughs and tears together. Nobody messed with us.

After my mother passed away, also from cancer, at a young age, my dad, who was also my hero, brought into my life a new mother with an additional sister and two brothers. Our families united and we had many parties and holidays together.

We never turned down the chance for a good meal. Above my front door, are the words: "Live Well, Laugh Often and Love Much". In life's journey I was blessed to experience all of these joys through my wonderful family and friends. These are my most important treasures.

I was so appreciative of the years I spent teaching. This has enabled me to find a remarkable group of women that became my very special friends in and out of this vocation. (You know who you are.) I love and appreciate you all so much. You are all very special to me.

I have never regretted not having children of my own. I had so many wonderful nieces and nephews to enjoy and many great students that I have been blessed to work with."

※

Charles Edward Frank

"Goodbye everyone that I have shared laughter, love and tears. I will miss you terribly. I have had a great life and it is time for me to go now, to the great fishing hole in Heaven. I was born 67 years ago with my twin Robert, to a loving family. Mom, Dad, Joe and former wife Peggy will be waiting for me when I arrive. Cancer and I had a fight and I won a trip to Paradise.

I proudly served my country in the US Navy. I have been many places, served many people and told many stories, some were even true! I stayed sober with the help of my Higher Power and AA for over 30 years.

I will miss playing cards with my buddies. More so, I will miss boating and fishing at Flaming Gorge every summer. Most of all, I will miss my family, Karla my fishing friend and loving wife; my two incredible sons, Edward B. and Michael C. (Merrilee); and my beautiful grandchildren, Edward C. and Samantha spoil them for me!

When you think of me, remember: Family, Friends and Fishing."

Robert E. "Bob" Nielsen

"To my loved ones: Well, for crying out loud, the day I have been studying for my whole life has finally arrived. Graduation! I am so tired of cramming for my finals, but now God has granted me the wish of my heart. The last two years were so long and confusing. My memory was robbed from me and then I lost my ability to be of service to others. Eventually I learned to let others serve me. God may even have taught me a little patience as I rocked in my chair each day. But, I never lost my love for visiting and joking around with family and friends (and playing with Lexi).

I want all of you to know how much I appreciated your visits. If I didn't know your name, I did know that you were an "angel." Especially my A-1 wife, Cora (Ida Red), and my daughters, Claetra and Nezla. It is hard for me to believe how much loving care they continually showed me even though I probably seemed like a stranger at times. Thank you, thank you.

Now to my family that I leave behind, and there are many, I say, "I am glad we shared this journey together. Please don't cry over my crowning achievement, keep smiling and celebrate this joyous occasion with me."

If a funeral has been planned, it is "over my dead body!"

Sorry Dad, but we are in charge now."

Lisa Mellenthin Randles

"I, Lisa Mellenthin Randles, age 40, passed away at my home in Layton, Utah, Nov. 29, 2005. Despite a year and a half battle with breast cancer, I left this world full of hope and love. I was born November 4, 1965 to Susan and Bill Mellenthin in Salt Lake City. Our mother, Susan Lynne Hogan, raised my sisters, Leslie and Nicole, and me. I also have a wonderful half- brother, Matthew Mellenthin, who was raised by my grandparents, Bill and Mary Mellenthin.

I am survived by my husband, John E. Randles: my best friend, my soul mate and the love of my life, as well as two amazing children, my daughter, Sierra Lynne (10) and my son, Kevin John (7). Together, the three of them have brought me more joy than I thought was possible in this life. I have been blessed with more true friends, special relationships, extended family, caregivers and loving supporters than almost anyone I know. Thank you, each of you, for the ways you have touched my life.

Please think of me when you think of reading, writing, learning and music. As long as you remember the things I love, a part of me will always be with you."

Vida Sue Hoffman

"Hi, my name is Vida, (pronounced like "Vita–min"). I was born in Lubbock, Texas on November 8, 1959. I graduated from Monterey High School in May of 1978, before settling in Nashville, Tennessee for 19 years. I attended UCLA where I earned my two- year certificate in Music Business. While in Nashville, I was blessed to meet many friends and have a vibrant life performing music for hundreds of people. I will always be grateful for the memories and moments.

I retired from Nashville and relocated to Salt Lake City in 2000. I was employed as a logistics trainer for Quest Diagnostics. I was blessed once again as my co-workers became my friends. With the love and support from many, I have been battling a rare ovarian cancer for 21 months.

A special thank you to all at Utah Cancer Specialists and Dr. Christopher Jolles for all that they do. My parents, Frankilene and Johnny W. Hoffman from Weatherford, Texas and my caregiver, companion and partner, LeAnna Porter and her daughter Aimee of Salt Lake City, survive me. I love you all."

Jill Marie Nielson

"My Soul Is Soaring. There I was. Mom and Merilee were pulling me one way, family and friends were pulling me another. I didn't know what to do or which way to go, I was ready to move on but I knew I was loved. My physical body was 55 years old and it only limited me, I was not very tall (short!!) and kind of round but I knew these people, they loved me and only wanted the best for me. I just knew I wanted to go home, my body said stay but my soul, my soul cried to be free. I wanted and needed to go home and here I am. Hey look at me now – I am tall and willowy."

Willis John Edgel
1928 – 2005

"I have been trying to think of a way to make my death easier on all of you. I want you to think of it this way. We are having another family campout. I have gone ahead to find a nice camping spot. The road is straight, but there are some rough spots along the way. Do not turn off the main road. At the end of the road you'll find a bend, I will be there waiting for you on the other side."

Willis John Edgel, 77, youngest son of John Francis and Maude Hillier Edgel, passed away Oct. 27, 2005 at home, after a long courageous battle with Pancreatic Cancer. He was born April 5, 1928 in the family home in Hoytsville, Utah."

Randy Pausch was an American professor of computer science when he learned he had pancreatic cancer in 2006. In August 2007 he was given a terminal diagnosis. On September 18, 2007 he gave an upbeat lecture titled "The Last Lecture: Really Achieving Your Childhood Dreams" at Carnegie Mellon. This lecture became a popular YouTube video and he appeared on numerous television and news shows as a result. He then coauthored a book called The Last Lecture on the same theme, which became a New York Times bestseller.

Randy Pausch
1960 – 2008

Last year, I agreed to give a last lecture at Carnegie Mellon University, where I'm a professor in the computer science department. A few weeks later, I learned that I had only months to live—I was dying of pancreatic cancer.

I knew I could cancel. I have three young children, I'm married to Jai, the woman of my dreams, and there were so many things to be done. But by speaking, I knew I could put myself in a bottle that would one day wash up on the beach for my children, Dylan, Logan and Chloe. Here's what I want to share.

Always Have Fun

Before I spoke, Carnegie Mellon's president, Jared Cohon, said to me, "Please tell them about having fun, because that's what I'll remember you for."

I came to an early realization. Each of us must make a decision; best captured in A.A. Milne's Winnie-the-Pooh characters. Am I a fun-loving Tigger or a sad-sack Eeyore? It's clear where I stand.

For my last Halloween, Jai, our kids and I dressed up as the Incredibles. I put a photo of us on my website and explained that chemo had not affected my superpowers. I got smiling e-mails in response.

I won't let go of the Tigger in me. Someone asked what I want on my tombstone. I said: "Randy Pausch: He Lived 30 Years After a Terminal Diagnosis." I could pack a lot of fun into 30 years. If that's not to be, I'll pack fun into the time I have.

Dream Big

I was 8 in the summer of 1969, when men first walked on the moon. I was at camp, and we campers were brought to the main house to watch the moment on TV. But the astronauts were taking a while, and it was late. The counselors sent us to our tents to sleep, and we missed the first walk.

I was peeved. I thought: "My species has gotten off our planet and is in a new world for the first time, and you people think bedtime matters?"

When I got home, my dad gave me a photo that he'd taken of our TV set the second Neil Armstrong set foot on the moon. We still have that photo.

Give yourself permission to dream. Fuel your kids' dreams too. Once in a while, that might even mean letting them stay up past their bedtimes.

Ask for What You Want

On a trip to Disney World, my dad and I were at the monorail with my son Dylan, then 4. Dylan wanted to sit in the nosecone with the driver, and my father thought it would be a kick too.

"Too bad they don't let regular people sit there," Dad said.

"Actually, I've learned there's a trick to getting to sit up front," I said. "Do you want to see it?"

I walked over to the attendant and said: "Excuse me. Could we please sit in the front car?"

"Certainly," the attendant said. He led us to the nosecone. It was one of the only times I ever saw my dad flabbergasted. "I said there was a trick," I told him. "I didn't say it was a hard trick."

Now I've gotten even better at "just asking." As we all know, it can take days to get medical results. Waiting is not how I want to spend my time, so I ask: "What's the fastest I can get these results?"

"Oh," they often respond, "we might be able to have them for you within an hour."

Ask. More often than you'd suspect, the answer you'll get is, "Sure."

Dare To Take a Risk

In a virtual – reality course I taught, I encouraged students to attempt hard things and not worry about failing. At the end of the semester, I presented a stuffed penguin—"The First Penguin Award"—to the team that took the biggest gamble while not meeting its goals. The award came from the idea that when penguins jump in water that might have predators, well, one of them's got to be the first penguin. In essence, it was a prize for "glorious failure."

Experience is what you get when you don't get what you wanted. And it can be the most valuable thing you have to offer.

Look for the Best In Everybody.

I got this advice from Jon Snoddy, my hero at Disney Imagineering. "If you wait long enough," he said, "people will surprise and impress you." When you're frustrated with people, when you're angry, it may be because you haven't given them enough time. Jon warned that this took great patience, even years. "In the end," he said, "people will show you their good side. Just keep waiting. It will come out."

Make Time for What Matters

When Jai and I went on our honeymoon, we wanted to be left alone. Since my boss demanded a way for people to reach me, I recorded this greeting:

"Hi, this is Randy. I waited until I was 39 to get married, so my wife and I are going away for a month. I hope you don't have a problem with that, but my boss does. Apparently, I have to be reachable." I then gave the names of Jai's parents and the city where they lived. "If you call directory assistance, you can get their phone number. And then, if you can convince my in-laws that your emergency merits interrupting their only daughter's honeymoon, they have our number." We didn't get any calls.

Time is all you have. And you may find one day that you have less than you think.

Let Kids Be Themselves

Because I've been so vocal about my childhood dreams, people have asked me about the dreams I have for my own kids. As a professor, I've seen how disruptive it can be for parents to have specific dreams for their children. My job is to help my kids foster a joy for life and develop the tools to fulfill their own wishes. My wishes for them are very exact and, given that I won't be there, I want to be clear: Kids, don't try to figure out what I wanted you to become. I want you to become what you want to become. And I want you to feel as if I am there with you, whatever path you choose."

Helen Kessler

"My name is Helen Kessler and I died on Sept. 20th 2009 from a biking accident. I had a great life and my heart was full of love for my Husband Brian and my son Zach and Prince the Fluffy dog. I will miss my mother Sally Garduno. My brothers Arnold Garduno his wife Phyllis, Vincent Garduno and his wife Lynn and my sister Esther Barney and her husband Richard, and all my nieces and nephews and cousins. Also to my extended family in California, Richard and Nancy White and their children, thank you for letting me into your life and family, you brought great joy to my life.

I had a chance to travel the world and experience all that it had to offer and to share that with my husband Brian and son Zach. For a little girl from Lark, Utah I was able to accomplish things in my life that even I could not foresee.

I was very fortunate to have been able to start my own business with my partners Peter Cooke and Mark Cohen. Together we started with nothing and over 25 years built PSC Development and Evergreen Management into one of the largest affordable housing company's in Utah. I will miss them and all the employees at both companies.

To my many friends, too many to mention, thank you for your friendship and love over the years. I will miss you all. When you can, think of me with a smile on your face, no tears. I have experienced many medical issues over my life, but I never let that stop me from doing the things I wanted to do or the things I wanted to accomplish. To the Doctors and Nurses at the University of Utah NCCU, and Dr. Skalabrin thank you for taking such good care of me, not all things can be fixed. So I leave now to join my brother Pete Garduno Jr. and my father Pete Garduno and I will wait for you. One day we will laugh again and love again.

Remember life is short and we do not know how much time we have, so live life as full as you can."

Hal G. Hardcastle

"I used to get up every morning and read the obituaries to see if I was still alive. Imagine my surprise this morning when I discovered I had slipped away from my family, friends and all my favorite places on Dec. 28, 2007. I was fortunate enough to be at home at the time surrounded by my loved ones. I'm certain this new trip I'm taking will be very exciting. I've always liked to go to new places. Well it looks like it was the cancers that finally got me, although I fought long and hard.

According to the legend, I was born on a dark and stormy night, the only child of Lucinda Mae Olsen and Thomas Harold Hardcastle. I spent my adventurous childhood in Sandy. I mooned a lot of trains, played on the beet dump and was even the President of Sandy Junior High. I moved into Salt Lake and graduated from South High in 1945.

While at the University of Utah I played a little football, but really enjoyed throwing the hammer for the track team. I graduated with a degree in education 1949 and a few days later on June 16th I married the love of my life, Marian Lois Fellows, she always looked great in bobby sox. Together we had three children, Cheryl Groot (Bill), Brett (Donna) and Tom. All three wonderful human beings who made me proud to be their dad. We also have two amazing grandchildren, Cathy and Jon Groot. I hope they know how proud I am of them and how much I love them.

I am a teacher. I guess the old adage is true, "A teacher is eternal; they never know where their influence stops. I loved the classroom but felt most fulfilled as a coach. During my time at Highland I was fortunate enough to be able to coach the most wonderful young men in the state including my own son Brett. I coached football, wrestling, cross-country and track and field. My sweetest memories of Highland are the days spent on the field with my teams. Hopefully I taught them more than the basics of the sport. They sure taught me a lot.

I will miss my many friends and associates; the poker group, the coffee buddies, the fishing and hunting friends, my golf and bowling partners and the many, many parties with so many friends.

I will also miss my backyard, my woodworking, the U of U football games and my volunteering. I am a flag-waving patriot and proud to have honorably retired as a Sergeant Major from the 96th US Army Reserve Command at Ft. Douglas after 29 years of dedicated service.

My thanks to the doctors who worked so hard to extend my life, Dr. Aslami, Dr. Eyring and Dr. Thorne. Without you and the team at the Huntsman Cancer Institute I never would have made it to my 80th birthday party. To Andrea and Juan of my team from Rocky Mountain Hospice, you're angels, thanks for making my last days ones of dignity and comfort."

Many individuals spend their lives in service to others, and this gives them the most satisfaction.

Elizabeth Cahn

"After my mother's death when I was eight years old, I was reared by an older sister who was a musician. She saw to it that I learned piano and acquired a musical education. During my high school years at Cuyahoga Falls High, I had a weekly radio program on WADC in Akron, and another accompanying a violinist on WJW.

After graduating from high school during the depth of the depression, I moved to New York City and got a job with a photography chain. I was promoted to "field girl," enabling me to travel between New York and Chicago. A mutual friend introduced me to the Rev. Horace "Mac" Martin McMullen and it was love at first sight. We enjoyed 55 years together, which included 11 years in Lebanon and Syria where Mac was President of the Near East School of Theology in Beirut, and later President of Aleppo College in Aleppo, Syria. We later returned to Beirut, where he served on the faculty of the American University of Beirut. While living in Beirut I attended Beirut College for Women.

I served as Adult Services Director for the YWCA of Salt Lake City for eight years, and served as a Caseworker for Congressman Wayne Owens and Congresswoman Karen Shepherd, handling Immigration and Veterans Affairs. I've loved dolls all my life and was an avid antique doll collector and member of the Olympus Doll Club. I was privileged to serve as President of the Salt Lake Doll Council. I've been an active member of PEO Chapter D since 1969, where I met many of my dearest friends."

She told the family gathered that "above all, love unconditionally and forgive."

Ruth Rich Coleman

"Life on earth has been a great experience for me. Born to Thair C. Rich and Cloteel Budge May 24, 1931 in Los Angeles, CA. My father was a career physician in the US Army Medical Corp so my formative years were spent in many areas of the United States, Panama, and Europe. This was a wonderful experience for my brother and me.

In 1954 I graduated from Catholic Univ. of America in Washington D.C. with a BSN. Returning to Salt Lake, I met and married the perfect mate for me – the optimistic, fun loving Jerry W. Coleman. Together, we raised Jeffrey, Janis and Karen. After the children began school, I returned to work in the nursing field for 30 years, retiring in 1998 from the Dept. of Dermatology at the Univ. of Utah.

My life has been fulfilling. A long and happy marriage, raising our children, the experience of being a grandmother, the many trips with friends and relatives, and most of all, the happy times at our home at Bear Lake. Our wonderful, caring daughters have always been there for me and the grandchildren have been the shining stars in my life.

A special thank you to friends, relatives, care givers at Care Source, Dr. Saundra Buys, and all who showed their love and support to me and my family. Until we meet again, Ruth."

❧

Andrea Estrada Santiago
"I was the oldest of seven children, and with that position in life I had a lot of responsibilities given to me. As a child when I went to school, I helped translate Spanish to English between teachers and students.

I married Julio Villa Santiago. We had a wonderful life together. We raised four children: three beautiful girls and a son, who is a gentleman, like his father. I was active in my church and loved to help with the cooking. I was instrumental in the start-up of LaMorena Cafe. I became a Eucharistic Minister of Our Lady of Guadalupe parish. My duties were to visit the sick and help see to their needs. In recognition of my work as a Eucharistic Minister, I was honored to receive a medal from Bishop Hunt, which I cherished!

I worked as a professional silk finisher. My specialty was wedding apparel. I took great pride and care in my job as I did with all my other duties in life. I enjoyed keeping busy and making things, such as crocheting for newborn babies and restoring dolls and stuffed animals for our church fundraisers.

I loved to help people and took pleasure in making new friends at the Northwest Senior Citizen Center. I had a great time with the company of everyone around me. I had many dear sweet friends, and I always appreciated their uplifting spirits."

❧

Robert O. Trottier

"I left for Paradise on May 28, 2008 to be with my family. I served in the U.S. Navy in World War II.

I love the LORD and His Church and my precious wife, Janette Platt. In life we were never separate and for Eternity we will be together. I love my special children and their spouses. My GRANDCHILDREN are the stars shining in my heaven.

I will miss my golf and bowling friends and the softball, fishing, hunting, and the beauties of this world. I was active in the LORD'S Church, devoting my life to Scouting, Family History and many callings. I estimated that I had extracted over a million names for Temple work.

I received Scouting's highest award, The Silver Beaver, after more than 60 years of service. "Life is Wonderful" was my slogan and when asked, I was always "WONDERFUL".

I have a place to rest my body in the Bountiful City Cemetery until Resurrection Morning"

❧

For many men, a life well lived included a life revolving around work and military service. Women might mention being a teacher or nurse, but men mention specific companies and organizations for which they worked.

Lt. Col. Roy C. Robinette

"Saturday, January 3rd was one of the most beautiful days of my life. A fresh snow had blanketed the Wasatch Front, and the sky reminded me of when I flew jets for the US Air Force.

I was blessed to spend one more moment with my sweetheart and best friend of 52 years, Carolyn, and my children. There have been many tears, laughter, prayers, and moments of my life I will cherish.

I wish to thank you all for your love and compassion. I especially wish to thank my lovely daughter Michelle for your tremendous faith and constant prayer and my son Steven for his strength and integrity. We sure did enjoy watching the U of U beat 'Bama in the Sugar Bowl. And also, thanks to my son Terry for his spirit and always making me smile.

I started my life on September 30, 1929, born to Roy C. Robinette Sr. and Clara Reynolds in Princeton, WV. I received my BS from Virginia Tech in Mining Engineering, and Masters in Aerospace Engineering at the University of Wyoming.

I served in the Vietnam War, and retired after 22 years in the Air Force. I continued to serve my country as a consultant for the Department of Defense for the remainder of my career.

My family means the world to me and I will continue to keep you in my prayers. Carolyn, my brother Louis and wife Natsuko, Steven and his wife Diane, Terry and his wife Lori, Michelle and her husband Mehran, and my grandchildren Nicole, Lauren, Christopher, Meggan, James, Anna, Taylor, Jonathan, and honorary son and Mac buddy, Jeremy.

I love you all. Please join me in a celebration of my life.

Fred G Cheney

"I retired in 2005 as Chief Financial Officer and a member of the Board of Directors after 41 years of service with Sentinel Security Life Insurance Company. During my career, I had the pleasure of working with a fine group of employees and formed many good relationships with many other professionals which I thoroughly enjoyed. I owe a great debt of gratitude to many people that were an important part of the Company, but I must offer a special thanks to Thomas W. Bartlett for the many years he and I served as officers. He was and, still is a good friend.

On May 17, 1994, I had the fortune to marry the love of my life, Teddy Staker, we were able to form a rewarding relationship that embellishes all that is important to happiness through understanding, love, sharing and the desire to spend quality time with each other. We loved to travel (especially cruising) and were fortunate to share many wonderful experiences. Teddy has qualities for a relationship that make me wonder how or why I was so lucky to have her for my partner. She always understood how to make life worth the goodness it can be. I'm only sad that we couldn't have had more time to continue our enjoyment of life together."

John L. "Jack" Roe

"My death was a result of bad health and good living. Believing as I do that when a person dies we lose a library, I was a husband, father and grandfather, an artist, wood carver, sculptor of stone, sailor (United States Navy Corpsman), para-archeologist, museum registrar, x-ray technician, photographer, historian, writer, hunter, lifetime NRA member, free mountain man, and avid fly and flat/saltwater fisherman.

I've buried some good friends and one good dog, and learned and forgotten countless times that life is a limited-time offer.

I was raised in Preston, Dubois, and Gooding, Idaho where I spent almost every waking moment on the Big and Little Wood Rivers. I was the oldest of three children, and made my own rules as many have seen me do. The family moved first to the Salt Lake City Rose Park area and then to Provo where I graduated from Provo High in the great year of 1957. Soon after, I joined the U.S. Navy. A year later I married my high school sweetheart, JoAnn Farrer of Provo, in Los Angeles, California, after she graduated (from Provo High). We were high school sweethearts.

Among other, lesser assignments, I was assigned to VF92 fighter squadron out of Alameda, California and was deployed to all five aircraft carriers, on the west coast at that time, and three Naval and Marine air stations before leaving the Navy in 1963.

We put our anchor down in Salt Lake City and then Murray, Utah, where we have spent the years raising five of six children, and I in pursuit of better hunting and bigger fish. I am survived by my wife and children, Shane (Ann) of Kearns; Patrick K. (Gaye) of Lehi; Taryn (Paul) Olds of Ogden; Mike A. (Kathy) of West Jordan; Josh L. of Murray; a mess of grand kids and great-grandkids, brother, Gary Roe and wife Darese; and the best friends a man can have.

Memorial services, or garden party, will be held in the outdoors surrounded by blue sky or even waterfowl weather! My ashes will be consigned partly to the side of my wife and soul mate, and the rest scattered at Flaming Gorge, or Wood Tick, Ferron Canyon. Family and friends will conduct the party. I'd like it to be a time to share memories and laughing and talking as though I'm still with you. I've always felt people could dress as they wanted, and always felt dressed up in skins or Levis and boots, shorts, tank tops and sandals. My family and friends are invited to wear their favorite, casual dress, western or other (skins?).

In lieu of flowers, I would suggest donations be made to Ducks Unlimited, the NRA, the Mule Deer and Elk Foundations, or the Nature Conservancy. Suit your fancy, or take a kid or good friend fishing, or to dinner – or both!"

Owen Urban Madsen

"See Ya, I didn't mean to leave you all so suddenly but I had to go. We had good times so remember them and begin to make new ones. You all knew me as Squirt, but was most proud of being a Grandpa whether I was related to you or not. I lived a good life by my standards and enjoyed boating, hunting, horseback riding, and most of all fishing.

I enjoyed my service to FOE 8235 and was a dual member of the Ogden Order for 55 years and the West Valley Order for 20 years. From 1945-1947 I enlisted in the Navy serving on the USS Arkansas, USS Henrico, USS Blue Ridge. My career was spent trucking, I was an owner/operator from 1969 and retired in 1990 working for PST.

I married Donna Street and into my life came our son Michael Lewis Madsen. We divorced and I found my sweetheart Eleanor "EL" Falk, with El she came two children Ken and Cathie who became mine and then we had a daughter, Jill. El passed on and a special friend Julie came into my life. I won't forget the special relationship with my grandson Dustin who helped me with the garden and became my helper and companion."

※

Olaf "Olie" Theodore Stevensen Jr.
"PAPA" BELOVED HUSBAND, FATHER, GRANDFATHER.

"On Saturday, May 30th, this Viking bought the farm! But, oh, what a great ride these 83 years have been. My loving children and grandchildren surrounded me when I moved on.

I attended East High School, where I pursued my passion for singing. Immediately thereafter, I was then inducted into the Army at Fort Riley, KS, followed by Cavalry duty at Fort Douglas, UT, where I also sang for the troops as a Special Forces member.

While "on leave," I bought a 50-cent ticket in a March of Dimes contest requiring a written response as to why one should contribute. My reward for 1st place was a 1946 Oldsmobile, which I sold so I'd have some "startup money" at War's end. And when that day arrived, I traded my nest egg for half interest in a hamburger stand that became Olie's Grill.

On July 28, 1948, I married the girl I'd followed home from school when I was 11 – Barbara Ann Arbuckle. During the next 40+ years, my sweetheart and I evolved our eatery into The 19th Green Club, Olie's Terrace Room, The Town House Athletic Club, and finally, The Salt Lake Athletic Club.

There was nothing Barb and I treasured more than spending leisure time with the family – whether it was sharing our love of music/singing or motor-homing and boating in the wilds.

My legacy was that they always remember "to stop and smell

the flowers." In the mid 80's, my wife and I launched three clothing boutiques in Utah and California.

After 57 years of marriage, my wife succumbed to a stroke in Fall 2005. Within hours, Susan and Mike welcomed me into their household where I was showered with "TLC"!

Having Sage, Lindsey, and Ashley begin and end each day with their kisses was "heaven." And when I wasn't enjoying long weekends at Shelley's, I was spending weeknights at local restaurants and movies with Shawn and Scott.

Don't mourn for me! I worked hard – but played even harder! While you read this, I'll most likely have located Barbara, upgraded to a new RV that's loaded with my favorite CDs, and am singing duets with her while we let "cruise control" steer us to whatever campgrounds the Universe has to offer!

To my family and all those who enriched my life – THANKS FOR THE MEMORIES. Love, Ted. In lieu of flowers, take someone special to lunch."

"P.S. Your family wants to THANK YOU, as well, for a lifetime of happiness and wonderful memories. You were a wonderful husband, great dad, and loving grandpa. Wherever we go, you and mom will always be with us!"

Robert H. Hinckley, Jr.
"In His Own Words"

"I was born lucky! As the first Hinckley grandchild, I was a birthday present for my Grandmother Hinckley. I was blessed with a sound and proud pioneer heritage.

I grew up in Ogden during the Great Depression. As a janitor at Robert H. Hinckley, Inc., I swept around a 1933 Dodge Sedan on the show room floor for 11 months before I finally sold it. While attending Ogden High School, I met a charming young lady by the name of Janice Scowcroft. I graduated from Ogden High School in 1936, attended Stanford University in 1937 and graduated from the United States Military Academy in 1942.

Life has been good for me, but the very best part of my life began eight years after high school, when I was able to convince Miss Scowcroft that this young Westpointer was the best teammate for her. Then came World War II, The Army Air Corps, B-24's, England, VE Day, and VJ Day, life in the Air Force and the Dodge automobile business in Salt Lake City.

Out of all of this quality time came four wonderful dividends in the form of great citizens: Robert H. Hinckley, III, oil analyst in New York City; James S. Hinckley, Dodge Dealer in Salt Lake City and Ogden; Dr. Scott S. Hinckley, owner of a small animal clinic in Anchorage, Alaska; Kristin H. Yeager, owner-operator of the Garden of Eden Welsh Pony and Arabian horse farm in Eden, Utah. What enormous dividends these great children have been.

I was born lucky. I lived lucky. I have had no problems in this world; I have had only opportunities. I have always had enough to eat, bags o'fun and great family experiences all with the finest teammate one could ever have – Janice Scowcroft Hinckley. We have loved each other and life together for 63 years.

Oh yes, I had the fun of enjoying nine of the friendliest Arabian horses that the breed has produced."

CHAPTER 5
Odds and Ends

Write Your Own Funeral — or as it's called these days — Your Celebration of Life.

If you are writing your own obituary, it makes perfect sense to plan your final send off as well. I have and update it regularly as new ideas appear or my tastes change. This truly is the last word on the subject of you. There are plenty of online sites to help you do just that.

MyWonderfulLife.com is a free on-line service to help you plan and personalize your own funeral so it reflects the way you lived. Preparing a one-page summary of your wishes, as well as other important information people need to know, will allow your loved ones more time to celebrate your life.

Whether you want a completely customized event, or a traditional funeral, websites and funeral homes stand ready to do just about anything you desire. There are many scenarios that can be fun to consider. Whatever you decide upon, it should reveal parts of your personality. Whowritesforyou.com has a complete complement of ideas.

- Are you a Trekkie? Full Star Fleet funeral.
- Do you want your ashes sailed out to sea in a Viking Funeral?
- Were you a traveler? Maybe you should be buried in your Tumi luggage?
- Do you have special music or readings you would like performed?
- Write down your favorite memories you love and want to share.

- Leave meaningful possessions to loved ones and tell them why
- Upload some of your favorite photos that can be used at your service.
- One good way to make sure your needs are met is to have regular Pallbearer Cocktail Parties to iron out the small details (more on that later).

Write your Own Exit

As I have had the opportunity to meet more and more people who are interested in this concept, not all have written their own obituary. But those who had some "advanced notice" as to their death wanted to have some control over their final days. The State of Oregon has installed the Death with Dignity Act (1997). As of 2009, more than 400 people have taken advantage of it. More information is available:

http://public.health.oregon.gov/ProviderPartnerResources/EvaluationResearch/DeathwithDignityAct/Pages/index.aspx

One special encounter was with Bernie Nolan. Her husband Roger used this option which empowers the dying person to be in control of the time of his or her death. They contacted Compassion and Choices (https://www.compassionandchoices.org/sslpage.aspx) who helped guide them through the necessary processes. Their granddaughter filmed and wrote a beautiful description of Roger and Bernie's experience.

TOASTMASTER SPEECH AT ROGER SAGNER'S FUNERAL BY ANGIE MOMIE

"Toast of Choice"

July 20, 2007 my 84-year-old grandfather killed himself.

And I filmed it.

I really have your attention now, don't I? But it's not what you might think.

Roger was the 343rd Unique American Citizen to take advantage of Oregon's Death with Dignity Act.

The law passed in Oregon in 1997 with a 60% margin – the ONLY state to do so until last year when Washington fought and won its battle.

Although this is a relatively new law, this is not a new need that humans have. Tradition holds that in nomadic Native American tribes, while moving to a new place, their old and dying would slowly drift from the pack and find a tree or a rock to sit by and wait to die. It was not considered inhumane, but considered an honorable and dignified way to die. In the spirit of **choosing** when not to burden their tribe any longer – the Native Americans enacted their own Death With Dignity tradition.

And Oregon has fought to continue it.

Now before I tell you about my grandfather, I'd like to give you some background on the law itself. To begin with, exactly what is Death with Dignity?

The official Oregon law verbiage is: DWD allows terminally ill Oregonians to end their lives through the voluntary self-administration of lethal medications, expressly prescribed by a physician for that purpose.

Basically, with a doctor's orders you may choose when to end your life.

However, you must qualify.

To qualify, two doctors must diagnose the patient as being terminally ill, with less than six months to live. That's very important – not just a terminal diagnosis, but less than six months to live.

In addition, both doctors must determine whether the patient is in sound mind and capable of making and communicating health care decisions for themselves. If either doctor feels this may be questionable – even if the question is depression – then the patient in required to undergo a psychological evaluation.

It is important to remember that the Oregon law is based on 100% autonomy – this is not Euthanasia – when the doctor administers the lethal dose – that is against the law. With DWD the patient self-administers.

In some cases, patients who receive a prescription do not use it – either they reconsider, lose their capacity to swallow the drug, or die of their underlying disease. Regardless, it provides the comfort of choice to the patient. Statistically in the eleven years this law has been in use, the total deaths are around 405-415, 2009 stats aren't in yet.

During 2008 specifically, 88 prescriptions were written, 54 actually used the medication. People who choose to end their lives this way generally had cancer and died at home under hospice care.

Which was exactly my grandfather's situation. Cancer had riddled his body. The once lively, strong willed, iconoclastic and **unforgettable** man had become a shadow of himself. And he knew it.

This was the type of guy who would fly to a far away place like Turkey, specifically NOT booking a hotel prior, for the pure adventure of having to figure out his self-created dilemma.

To him, life was not about quantity – it was about quality. And when that quality went away, he chose to take control of the situation and end it on his own terms.

The night before I got a call from my grandma saying "Roger is killing himself tomorrow." We're a very matter of fact family. For her it was mixed emotions of grief and relief. The constant care of a crotchety old man who knew he was dying took a toll on her love for him and happiness in her own life.

I was frozen by the news – not because I was surprised – we all knew this was coming but I had mixed feelings on it. He was STILL Roger.

Still fun to talk to and learn from. And frankly, I didn't know how to feel. As my Aunt Brenda said "No one really knows how to deal with the 'putting to rest' of someone – the only reference is putting a pet to sleep but you don't want to pat Roger on the head and give him a treat." There is really no script for this situation.

Which is why despite Roger saying he didn't want anyone there – being the family we are – no one could stay away.

And you know what? It turned into one of the most beautiful and calming situations I have ever been a part of.

The whole family came. The volunteers from Compassion and Choice of Oregon were there. And as the volunteers began to tear apart the 100 individual capsules of Seconal to be dissolved into water, we asked them why they were part of this movement. One man had watched his mother and wife both starve themselves in Seattle hospital beds to die faster. He said, "no one should have to die that way."

Neither did Roger.

As the hour approached, we began to gather around my grandfather's hospital bed in the living room. We let him run the show and he was king for a moment. He gave each of us in turn parting words of wisdom bringing tears to our eyes – we joined him in signing his favorite song "My Way" and then, being a lifelong Republican, he went on a tirade about how amazing President Bush was – which wasn't the most wonderful part, but it was him.

He got to be Roger Sagner in full color, and with an audience, for the remaining moments of his life. He died as he loved to live.

At this point Roger asked our compassion volunteer, if she would be writing about him. She said, no, and he seemed disappointed so she asked him if he'd like to be part of a documentary film about this subject. He said "Of course!" Roger was a total ham and would be the perfect candidate. She unfortunately could not get a hold of the filmmaker in time so I said, "I'll do it." Not knowing just how difficult that might prove to be.

So I got the video camera and starting filming things – people, expressions, the song, the words, Roger.... then it was time.

I said "I don't wanna watch this" – as I never planned on watching the actual send off and tried to hand the camera to my technically challenged Aunt who said she would take it but as she quickly proved incapable of using it, so I took it back and continued to film as our compassion volunteer asked him the three final questions before handing him the medication. She ended with "You have the right to change your mind. Do you wish to do so?" He answered a resounding "Hell no" and took the glass from her.

He then starting singing a song that haunted me for months:
*"I'm coming, I'm coming, for my head is bending low,
I hear them gentle voices calling Old Black Joe."*

And I watched him through a lens as he drank and laid down, still singing the words "I'm a comin' " until he fell into a deep sleep. It took less than five minutes for his heart to stop. He was ready.

The mood in the room was not one of sadness. One of loss, yes, but we were all stunned at the civilized and dignified way it unfolded.

It felt right.

I remember feeling proud of Oregon and my grandfather as they lifted his draught of freedom saying and I quote "I thank the wisdom of the voters of Oregon for allowing me the honor of doing myself in at my own volition."

Fellow Toastmasters, what will be your dying toast? What will you want to say? I hope you have the choice to determine that.

Oregon Law: Death with Dignity

THE LAW:
Roger and I both voted for the Oregon Law both times it was on the ballot. From the beginning he saw that having some (dignity) when death got too close was a good thing. We knew the law existed, but we did not have a lot of information. I had some more information because I helped my grandson write a paper about it for his Social Issues Class.

TERMINAL DIAGNOSIS: (March 2007)
During December of 2006 Roger started having a series of medical problems. He had unexplained fevers, trouble with his bowels, new aches and pains. After a series of doctor's appointments that ruled out infections in his chest or urinary infections, we feared that his prostate cancer was causing the trouble. We already knew that the cancer had spread to the bone. We had gone to an oncologist at that time. He said there was nothing to be done until the cancer became symptomatic. By February we knew that cancer was the problem. The oncologist confirmed that Roger was in the final months of his life.

INFORMATION: (March 2007)
Roger had time to come to grips with the information. He had lived with cancer for 16 years. Since 2002 his PSA had been raising, so we knew that cancer was active. It still could be put on the back burner for a while. After a radiation treatment that made him very sick, he was ready to get more information on the Oregon Law. Earlier he had researched the Hemlock Society and had asked his doctor about death by starvation. He was determined to have some control.

Hospitals and doctors are either reluctant or don't know the details of the Oregon Law. It was lucky that a social worker put Roger in touch with Compassion and Choices. Roger made a phone call and got the information from the phone call and was later mailed brochures.

FIRST STEP: (March 2007)
Roger learned that he had to make a request to his doctor and the doctor had to fill out a form documenting the request. That request had to be followed up by a second request at least 15 days later. His Primary Care Doctor was very understanding and just followed Roger's request. He had seen Roger's new PSA of 1000 and agreed that the cancer was taking its toll. He also verified that Roger was mentally competent. As with most doctors, he had little actual experience with the law. He had ordered at least one other prescription.

SECOND DOCTOR: (April 2007)
Because Roger's oncologist had already told us that Roger was in his last months, we took the form for verification for him to fill out and sign. He was willing to verify Roger's diagnosis. He did let us know that he would not be the prescribing physician. He also said that Roger did not have to make another appointment with him.

NEXT STEP: (April 2007)
At the next appointment Roger had with his Primary Care Doctor, he turned in the form from the oncologist and made a second request for the prescription. Roger was not the least bit hesitant at this time. He had made up his mind that he wanted the pills available. He did not know if he would use them or not.

COMPASSION VISIT: (May 2007)
Roger thought he had completed all of the necessary paperwork. The compassion volunteer came on a counseling visit and let him know that there was still another form that he had to fill out. This form required signatures from two witnesses that knew Roger. Roger filled it out and it was witnessed. I took the form to his Primary Care Doctor's office. Roger had decided to wait a while before the prescription was sent to the pharmacy.

DR. SENT PRESCRIPTION TO THE PHARMACY: (June 2007)
Roger could feel his condition worsening. He feared his swallow reflex, his weakness, and some mental confusion. He called his Primary Care Doctor and asked to have the prescription sent. We found out that it would take the pharmacy 2 weeks to fill the order because they did not have the pills on hand.

PRESCRIPTION PICK-UP: (July 10, 2007)
When Roger found out that his prescription was in, he had James drive him to get it. He thought he had to be present to pick up the prescription. I'm not sure what the rules are around this.

CALLED COMPASSION: (July 18, 2007)
Roger said that he had nothing left and he called and made an appointment for someone from Compassion and Choices to come on the following Friday.

DEATH WITH DIGNITY: (July 20, 2007)
Roger celebrated his last day.

Shoot Your Own Obituary Photo

As you can see from the back cover of this book, anybody can take a picture these days. We have smart phones and smart cameras and computers that can handle these functions. And if you aren't quite sure you like the way you look, you can Photoshop it "to death". (Please excuse the pun.)

Your Final Resting Place
In the Ground – Green vs. Steel

Over the years my feelings have changed from a traditional burial to cremation, and I have toyed with the idea of a green burial. This article lays it out pretty plainly the cost of a our traditional funerals on the environment and pocketbook.

"Dying to Be Green"
by Neil Shea, National Geographic Magazine,
July 2008. Environment Section:

"Death, it turns out is bad for the environment. The end of life is often followed by the start of the process steeped in toxic embalming and marked by the consumption of resources – a U.S. funeral typically costs about $6,000. One alternative is the green burial movement, which began in England in the 1990's and has since spread around the world. Embalming is skipped (it's usually not required by law unless there's a long delay or the body crosses certain state lines. Biodegradable materials like paper are used for shrouds, coffins and crematory urns.

The burial site matters too, says Joe Sehee, founder of the Green Burial Council. A growing number of cemeteries cater to clients who want their remains to return to the earth beneath land uncluttered by headstones or mausoleums. Brenda Proffitt of Albuquerque, New Mexico and her husband recently bought plots in a green cemetery in the high desert. Like many of the graves, theirs will be unmarked. A GPS device will record the location beside a boulder and a few pines. She likes the idea of returning to ancient no-frills burial traditions while embracing her 21st century values.

Gone Forever

Burial inters more than a body. Below, a roundup of what else goes under in the U.S. each year.
- 30 million board feet of casket wood, including tropical hardwoods
- 90,000 tons of steel – more than enough to build the Golden Gate Bridge

- 1.6 million tons of concrete in burial vaults
- Over 80,000 gallons of embalming fluid, more than enough to fill an Olympic-size pool."

In the Water or the Wind
(Legal places to scatter your ashes.)

Kathleen Mulvaney, an eHow contributor, offered her own "Memorial Ideas for Spreading Ashes"

"An increasing number of people are opting to have their deceased loved ones cremated instead of choosing a traditional burial service. Proper storage is required from the time the ashes are collected to the time they are scattered. Some people believe that the method of scattering a loved one's ashes determines where the person spends his afterlife. Choosing a proper site for scattering the ashes is important in the preservation of the soul of the departed.

Certain techniques can be applied when opting to bury the ashes to ensure proper disposal of the remains. "Raking" involves scattering the ashes atop soil and using a rake to immerse the ashes back into the earth from where they came originally. "Trenching" involves digging a hole in the ground, disposing of the ashes and then covering the remains with soil. The ashes can either be placed directly into the trench or into a biodegradable urn to be buried along with the ashes.

Often, loved ones want to scatter the ashes in a location cherished by the family. A favorite childhood spot, a sports venue or a wooded area can serve as a location for the scattering of ashes. For both public and private locations, always check with the landowner before disposing of the ashes. Ashes can be harmful to the environment, and proper disposal is necessary.

The ocean, a lake or ponds are three options for scattering ashes in a body of water. Some people believe that disposing of ashes into a body of water creates a final separation between the soul and the body, allowing the deceased to fully pass on into the afterlife. When choosing a body of water to dispose of the ashes, seas make an ideal choice due to their all-assimilating power. If you cannot get to a sea, though, any flowing body of water will do. It is best to also dispose of the urn along with the ashes. This prevents you from holding on to any negative energy that may be associated with the ashes. Memorials can be created in cemeteries when ashes are scattered in water, so that loved ones have a place to go and honor the deceased.

Disposing of ashes in the sea creates a separation between the body and the soul. You can scatter ashes three miles from the shoreline"

www.affinitycremation.com offers the following advice for land distribution: "We suggest that you think of the cremated remains as being your own private property. You would not be allowed to deposit your private property on public lands, parks, lakes, etc. or on someone else's property without their consent. The same restrictions apply to cremated remains... Scattering on your own private property or the private property of another who has given you permission is acceptable. We recommend obtaining this permission in writing.

Scattering over public lands (i.e., state parks, county or city parks, beach, etc.) is not usually permitted without the expressed permission from the appropriate governmental agency with authority over the site.

Scattering of ashes is permitted within many popular national parks with a **Special Use Permit.** For more information on scattering ashes within a national park, please contact the National Park Service. Most parks charge a small fee for this permit.

You may wish to consider the use of a biodegradable urn, which may be buried in the ground and is designed to decompose underground providing for a completely eco-friendly burial."

Some families may choose to have their loved one's ashes scattered by a pilot during a flight. There are airplanes specifically designed for the purpose of scattering ashes, and the pilot is in charge of disposing of the ashes and alerting the loved ones the time and the place the aerial scattering will occur.

www.celestis.com offers Memorial Spaceflights, where they "place a symbolic portion of cremated remains into Earth orbit, onto the lunar surface, and into deep space. Missions into space that return the cremated remains to Earth are also available. Your loved one will venture into space as part of a real space mission, riding alongside a commercial or scientific satellite.

Memorial Spaceflights are made possible through agreements with leading providers of commercial space launch services. All services include a performance assurance guarantee."

These shuttles leave at least annually, and if you look at the website you can see who has already signed up for a future flight.

In a Jar – Fire vs. Ice

We are all familiar with cremation. It's been around for decades. More people choose cremation than the traditional burial, but there is a new form of burial that **freeze-dries** the body with liquid nitrogen. The Swedish company, Promessa, which describes it as an environmentally friendly alternative to conventional burials and cremations, developed it. Burials can lead to underground watercourses becoming polluted, while cremations give rise to harmful mercury emissions from tooth fillings.

These types of burials will begin within the next year in Sweden. For Scotland the issue is land — an effort to free up space in overcrowded cemeteries. The "promession" technique means a person's remains can be absorbed into the soil within months instead of decades, freeing up burial plots in graveyards that are running out of space for the 55,000 Scots who die every year.

European environmental laws require all UK crematoriums must cut their emissions of mercury by 2012, and promession is the best solution said Susanne Wiigh-Mäsak, the Swedish biologist who devised promession. "Many people find this a very appealing idea. It takes the best from burial and the best from cremation," she said.

Under promession, the body is slowly frozen to -18C then submerged in liquid nitrogen at -196C before being vibrated until it shatters. The water is then evaporated, to allow fillings, hip joints, pacemakers and other metals to be removed, leaving a pile of powder roughly a third of the weight of the deceased.

The remains are then buried in a small biodegradable starch coffin in a shallow grave, where there is more oxygen, animal and bacterial activity that turn the contents into compost in six to 12 months. After testing the process on dead pigs, the Swedish health board approved it last year. The town of Jonkoping is now building the world's first "promatorium" and parish councils in the country have been inundated with inquiries.

The world's first promession ceremony is expected in Sweden within a year. As yet, this type of procedure is not available in the United States.

Are you a Diamond in the Rough?
(might as well turn your carbon into jewelry)

There are countless ways to memorialize a loved one, but probably none as unusual as turning your ashes into a diamond.

LifeGem Memorial Diamonds (www.LifeGem.com) can turn your loved one's ashes into authentic and certified diamonds. Depending on the type of diamond and jewelry you desire, prices can range up to $19,000 per piece. Their website states that 4,000 have chosen to have their loved one's carbon made into pieces of jewelry, and over 3 million people have viewed their site.

If you don't want to send your loved one off to LifeGem, eHow.com has a step-by-step instruction sheet on how to create a jewel from your loved one:

"Degree of Difficulty: Very Challenging.

Things You'll Need:
- Crucible
- Core
- Metal catalyst
- Seed crystal
- Diamond press
- Faceting tools
- Ash

Step 1. Place several ounces of ash in a crucible that can withstand massive heat.

Step 2. Bring the temperature to just over 5,000 degrees Fahrenheit, and allow all of the elements except the carbon to oxidize.

Step 3. Continue to heat until the carbon has turned to graphite. The entire heating process will take a few weeks.

Step 4. Place the graphite in a core with a metal catalyst and a diamond seed crystal.

Step 5. Place the core in a diamond press.

Step 6. Bring the temperature to about 2,500 degrees Fahrenheit and the pressure to about 800,000 pounds per square inch. Allow several weeks for the graphite to turn into a rough crystal.

Step 7. Remove the crystal and use faceting tools to cut it to your specifications.

Get Under Someone's Skin as a Tattoo

Considered the ultimate form of memorializing a deceased loved one by some, using cremation ashes in a memorial tattoo has been done. You will run into several obstacles when pursuing this venture including refusal by many tattoo artists and several health-related concerns. Do your homework before making the decision to include someone's bodily remains in a tattoo. But just in case you do, eHow.com has step-by-step instructions for preparing the ashes for tattooing. Here is some of their discussion:

"Degree of Difficulty: Moderately Challenging.

1. Prepare ashes for tattooing. When a body is cremated, the residual bone matter will not be a fine dust but more like small pebbles or a sand-like substance. You need to sift out the larger pieces to glean just the finest particles to mix in the tattoo ink. There are some who have also found various ways to grind the entire remains into a finer powder.

2. Bake the ashes prior to use. It's been suggested that you bake the cremation ashes you'll be using in order to "sterilize" them. However, it's also been said the temperature at which the body is cremated should have eliminated any germs or diseases that might have been present in the body. You'll be hard pressed to find any scientific information about the validity of either claim.

3. Search for a tattoo artist willing to use cremation ashes in a tattoo.

Because of the uncertainty of the advisability of introducing these foreign bodies into your skin and the lack of experience in adding cremation ashes to tattoo ink and then using it in the tattoo, many tattoo artists are going to be hesitant to do the procedure.

Tips & Warnings

If you decide to exclude the ashes, you can still get a wonderful memorial for your loved one permanently inked on your skin."

Outlived Your Family and Friends?
Hire Professional Mourners

Professional Mourners are as old as time. Mentioned in the Bible, the occupation is widely invoked in literature, from the early centuries BC to modern poetry.

Funeralsite.com describes Professional Mourners as people, usually women, who are paid to attend and mourn at a funeral. This practice has largely disappeared from Western culture, but still thrives in Eastern cultures. Here is a recent article on one such woman in China.

"Professional Mourners Spice Up Traditional Funerals in China
By Sebastien Blanc, AFP, Jun 17 2011

CULTURE: Chinese tradition dictates that the children and grandchildren of the dead must express their grief in a noisy manner, and with plenty of tears, before the burial. Hu Xinglian kneels before the corpse of Liang Zhicai and, with one hand on his metal coffin, lets out a piercing wail. But Hu is not at all grief-stricken — she is a professional mourner.

In parts of China, where rural preburial rituals are still observed, mourners known as "kusangren" are hired to guarantee that a funeral is a spectacle in grief. And the 53-year-old Hu is up to the task. She comes to work with a full sound-system, multicolor spotlights and the six members of her band, "The Orchestra of the Star and River of Chongqing … She and her band eat dinner al fresco with the family — washed down with ample quantities of Sichuan beer. Hu then dons a full white robe — the color of mourning in China. Liang's relatives kneel around the coffin, their eyes fixed on Hu as her wails reach a fever pitch ... Hu then dances for several minutes, falling to her knees and crawling several times before shaking the hands of the visibly moved family members. And then suddenly, the evening turns festive. Funereal chants are replaced with popular songs and comedy stories. A belly dancer performs, followed by a woman in a leopard-print bustier, black leather hot pants and fishnet stockings who writhes to a pulsating techno beat."

So do we have actors, belly dancers and strippers available here in the states?

Not exactly, though modern funeral homes can handle nearly every facet of your final celebration. They can do everything from supplying someone to deliver the eulogy, hiring seat fillers and professional pallbearers and can even rent suitable clothing for the family to wear.

Many funeral homes have been in the family for decades. But that doesn't mean they are old and staid. Check out the website for the Kuhn Funeral Home, www.kuhnfuneralhome.com, which has been serving their community since 1937. In addition to traditional affairs, they also offer the Celestis Program, which launches cremated remains into outer space, and the Eternal Reefs Program in which your cremated remains are made into an ocean reef. They even offer house sitters. So if you need a belly dancer to assist on your "transition from this mortal coil" it appears it requires no more than finding a funeral home that matches your desires with their services.

Have Friends and Family to Choose From?
Choose from attendees at a Pallbearer Party.

So what exactly are Pallbearers and where did the term come from?

eHow.com describes them "as those who help carry the casket of the deceased at a funeral."

Wikipedia states that the name is derived from a pall, which is the heavy cloth that is draped over a coffin. The term "pallbearer" describes someone who bears the pall.

In western cultures, the pallbearers are usually associated in an intimate manner with the deceased before their death. In some Asian cultures, pallbearers are not members of the family but are outsiders, paid to perform the services.

How did the Craig C. Dunford Pallbearer Group come to be?

I guess I have always thought a little outside the box and so I wondered who said pallbearers had to be male? Women, I want women to carry me to my final resting place. After all, it was a woman, my beloved Mother, who carried me into this world. So why not have women carry me out? I have always liked women. No, I love women. I enjoy the way they smell, look, talk, interact, make things happen and take pleasure in one another's company. I just think women are the best!

As I think about the seven women I have chosen to be my pallbearers I realize they all have a great deal in common. They are all smart, funny and strong in body, mind, and spirit. They are also spontaneous, brave, creative and passionate about so many things. These women like animals and kids. They have all experienced death up close and personal. They have lost parents, some at a very young age, spouses, siblings, children, animals, and friends. None of them are afraid to talk about the difficult things. They also think outside the box. They can embrace both the joy and sorrow of life.

I really cannot tell you how they all came to be my pallbearers. It was not like I sat down with a yellow legal pad and made a checklist of characteristics these women would have to possess. Some I have known for almost 40 years, none less than 20. It happened spontaneously and with little effort. They just came to me and I made a heartfelt connection with each and every one of them. We all speak the same language. They are part of "my family of choice". They are in my TRIBE.

I didn't plan it this way, but am comforted by the fact I ended up with " a doctor, a lawyer, a merchant chief"... along with teachers, artists, musicians, a realtor, several philanthropists and just all around great women. I've got all my bases covered. Too bad I will be dead. I'll miss being physically with them for our Pallbearer (wine-tasting, food loving, spirited conversation) events. I certainly hope we will still have some connection after this life is over.

I have enjoyed our group and individual meetings throughout the years and feel they have all enriched my life immensely. The fact that my wife loves them too is another bonus.

TAM

I first met Tam when she and her sister ran "Mother's Earththings". If you remember hippy clothing you will get how cool that place was. Leading edge.

Seared into my brain were her sparkling eyes. Her personality matched the eyes. That was around 1964. She really never changed. Beautiful, confident, energetic, entrepreneurial, and maybe above all else genuine. If you ever need an honest real estate representative, she is your person.

MJ

My addled brain is chronologically challenged. I think MJ is next in the sequence. Mitzi and I, as a young couple, started out living in a cute, cheap, old Mormon (read here polygamist) house. Two stories held 4 apartments. We in the upper North, MJ and Jim in the lower South. We were young, they were younger. I remember they had the best cat I'd ever seen. Not a cat lover, I'd never seen a cat that would come when you called. One of my fondest memories was the day my cousin and I were moving something heavy into my place. MJ was "laying out" on the front lawn in an untied bikini. Can't have those unsightly lines. As we approached, she was somewhat startled and sprang to her knees to secure her top. As fate would have it, her tender fingers could not hold the massive force being applied to the fabric, and it sprang loose across her chest and over her shoulder. Being Mormons at the time, we were sure that this was one of those blessings they talk about. MJ, Mitzi, and I go pretty far back, that was about 1970. Then as now, she was one of the smartest cute ladies I've ever encountered. She is one great tattoo artist, and a superb humanitarian as well. If you go to the Portland area, just ask about anyone on downtown streets if they know Mary Jane Haake ..... they'll know.

ALYCE

Originally, was a school mate of my sisters. Not known until years later. I did go to college with the guy who would eventually become her husband. His family was quite well-to-do, and Kent made a wise choice when it came to Alyce. She has always been a very classy human. In my mind, she ended up as a very real and caring person that could "rub shoulders" with all social levels of people. She is one who has all of the things of life, and has moved on to use her talent and influence to benefit others. A perfect example was the blanket that her friends made for her when she encountered a serious illness. It was made from cloth remnants that had special meaning to each person. She recovered and proceeded to use that blanket to heal many others; my wife included.

SALLY

Best I know, our sons became friends before we did. Lucky us. Mitzi knew of Sal through A Women's Place Book Store. She was a great owner, and contributed a lot back to our community. When I got to know her personally it was easy to see why she was such a successful, well-read, bubbly, open, embracing-of-life Mom/ Grand Mom/Wife. She has the most interesting perspective on all subjects, and became an extraordinary english teacher. Not to mention that she is a "stand up" kind of person.If you know the candid TV show where injustices are committed in public with a hidden camera. She'd be the one that every time would step in and confront the wrong-doer. I wish I could say that I have that kind of fortitude.

MATTY

Matty married a guy that was my twin brother in another life. At least I thought so. Mitzi was her sorority "mother" or whatever they are called. We had kids about the same age, and spent some great vacation times together. She has survived more than her share of lifetime challenges, but was superb at making the lemons taste great. She became an excellent lawyer, and is now with a great guy (even if she can beat him at golf). Through good times and not so good, she remained a great Mom. Is still very close with her kids and their kids, and some step kids along the way. Even with "silver" hair she looks classically younger that her years. Fit, cute, athletic, fun, funny, she is just great to be around.

MARJORIE

My old high school pal, and my interest in end of life issues lead me to Marjorie. When we and they were alive (her spouse and my friend now gone) she was the caregiver to a man of incredible qualities. She dearly loved him. He had MS and she single handedly carried them both, and their children through the whole ordeal. He was a beer aficionado, she supplied the straw when that was the only way he could consume any. That talent was as big as her artistic talent. Not only a very successful selling artist in many mediums, she is also a superb teacher of that subject. She is like Mother Nature living amongst us (you should see her garden!!!). Envision someone who can please the visual senses, and care for the sentient beings.

JULIE

Once more my wife opens this door. Her former business partner and a cute new ER Doc. that worked with her sister were both single... Mitzi couldn't stand that and "Yentled" (I know that's not a word, but you get the idea) them together. We all met on various occasions, and I got to find what a smart - strong - golfer - Capt. Morgan-drinker - have funner - computer wizard - caring horse person (dressage), not to mention skilled doctor she was. I admit it, I was madly in love. Her now husband said that they needed my OK before they could marry. I'm glad I finally gave it. They are a great couple, and better friends.

CHAPTER 6
Miscellaneous Reflections

Obituaries can show us what is really important in our own lives; pass on wisdom and our most heartfelt ideas, and allow us to express sincere feelings to those important to us. Shared personal stories, especially those that come from our true selves are a priceless gift, and can improve the quality of our experiences and relationships.

Excerpts from a story by Dick Polman (Knight Ridder News) about the death of Francois Mitterrand:

"He is dying now, and only massive doses of morphine can dull the pain. His few remaining friends doubt that he will survive until Christmas. But they know he will not resign. They know he cannot accept the idea that anyone else could be president of France."

"At age 77, he is trying to write his own obituary while he still breathes. Yet, curiously, he doesn't seem to mind that some of the facts are quite damning."

"All of Mitterrand's life has been a desire for power. And power is good for sick people. Power is exciting; power is life; power gives them hope. And if they lose it, there is nothing else to live for."

༄

Billy Graham at Richard Nixon's funeral:

"John Donne once said that there is a democracy about death. It comes equally to us all and makes us all equal when it comes."

༄

Excerpts from Peggy Fletcher Stack's article (S.L. Tribune) Death of a Child:

"That day time did not stop for the passing of our child. We had trouble forgiving the universe for taking so little note of so great a loss... For two years, our normal life had been caring for our terminally ill child. 'Camille was like a magic jewel making everything around her glow.' Mike said to me, after one such comment. 'Who wouldn't exchange a magic jewel for a good night's sleep?' One day, Suzanne found me crying. 'Why are you sad, Mommy?' she asked. 'I miss Camille, honey.' I told her. 'You still have Karren, and Jamie, and me.' she said, nestling in my arm. I realized then that no matter how we felt, we could not let our sorrow for Camille outweigh our joy for our three living children."

☙

Judith S. Johnessee (Associated Press) Your cat is dying.

MAMARONECK, N.Y. – I am not sure how he got to my clinic. He did not really look old enough to drive, although his child's body had begun to broaden and he moved with the heavy grace of young manhood. His face was direct and open, and when I walked into the waiting room my first view was of him consciously and lovingly petting his cat through the open door of the carrier on his lap. With a schoolchild's faith in authority, he had brought his sick cat in for me to fix and sat waiting with patience and confidence.

The cat was about the boy's own age, give or takes a year, but she was a tiny thing. I could see how her spots and stripes and her fierce, bright face had evoked the image of a tiger in a child's mind, and Tigress she had become. She was an exquisitely formed cat with a delicate skull and beautiful markings. Age had dimmed the bright green fire of her eyes into faded lace but she still was elegant and self-possessed and she greeted me with a friendly rub against my hand.

I began to ask questions, trying to determine what had brought this charming pair to see me, and the boy answered them simply, directly and honestly, unlike most adults who dissemble, ramble or tell you everything but the answer to the question you actually asked. In a matter of minutes I learned that Tigress had had a normal appetite until recently, that several days ago she had begun to vomit a couple of times a day, and now she was not eating at all and had become withdrawn from her human family.

My mental computer did not come up with anything obvious from this history, so I petted and stroked Tigress and told her how beautiful she was while I examined her eyes and mouth, listened to her heart and lungs, and palpated her abdomen. My fingers found it. A tubular mass in her mid–abdomen. Tigress politely tried to slip from my searching fingers. She did not like the mass being handled. She also had lost a pound, which is a lot when you only weigh 6 pounds.

I looked at the fresh-faced youngster and back at the cat he had probably had all his life. I was going to have to tell him that his most beloved companion had a mass, probably a cancer, in her abdomen. Even if her mass were surgically respectable, she probably would live less than a year, and she might need weekly chemotherapy to get even that. It would all be difficult and expensive. So I was going to have to tell this child that his cat was going to die. And there he was, all alone.

Death is something that is pushed to the background and ignored as long as possible, but in reality every living thing one loves will die. It is an omnipresent part of life. How the first death is experienced can be life-forming. Death can be an unbearable thing of horror and suffering, or a peaceful release. I wondered why this child was here alone. I would have to guide him through this myself. I was tired from the long morning. I did not want this burden. It had to be done perfectly or this child, who was not even mine, might end up emotionally scarred.

It would have been so easy just to leave the room and call a parent and discuss this all with them and shirk this onerous task. But when I looked at his direct and open face, I could not do it. I had spent too long palpating the horror that was eating away at Tigress' life, and he knew something was wrong. I could not just ignore him and call his parents and have them explain it all to him. It would have been cruel. So I talked to him as Tigress' rightful owner and told him as gently as I could what I had found and what it meant. As I spoke he jerked convulsively away from me, probably so I could not see his face, but I had seen it begin to twist even as he turned.

I sat down and turned to Tigress, to give him some privacy, and stroked her beautiful old face with my fingers while I discussed his alternatives with him. They are the same old unchanging options for bad disease – put her through the extensive presurgical work-up and then attempt to remove and run a biopsy on the mass, let her continue to fade away at home or give her an injection and put her to sleep. He listened carefully and nodded gravely. He said he did not think she was comfortable anymore and he did not want her to suffer. He was trying hard. The two of them broke my heart. I offered to call a parent to explain what was going on.

Somewhat relieved he gave me his father's number in the city. I went over everything again with the father while the boy stood and listened and petted his cat. Then I let father speak to the son. The child paced and gestured and his voice broke a few times, but when he had hung up he turned to me again with dry eyes and said only that they had decided to put her to sleep. No rage, no denial, no hysteria – just rational acceptance of the inevitable. I could see, though, how much it was costing him.

I asked him if he wanted to take her home overnight to say good-bye. I thought she was stable enough to give him this time to get used to the awful news I had given him so suddenly. But he just said no, he just wanted to be alone with her for a few minutes. I left them alone and went to sign out the barbiturate I would use to ease her into a painless sleep. I could not control the tears that were streaming down my face, or the grief I felt welling up inside of me for this child who had had to become an adult so quickly and so alone.

I waited outside the exam room. In a few minutes he came out and simply said he was ready. I asked him if he wanted to stay with her. He looked surprised, but I explained that it often was easier to see how peaceful it was than to forever wonder how it actually happened. Seeing the logic of that, he held her head and reassured her while I administered the injection and she drifted off to sleep, her head cradled in his hand.

The animal itself always looked quiet and at rest. The owner now bore all the suffering. This was the finest gift you could give to something you loved, to assume their pain that they might rest. He nodded. He understood. Something was missing though. I did not feel like I had completed my task. It came to me suddenly that though I had asked him to become a man instantly, and he had done so with grace and strength, that in essence he still was a child.

I held out my arms and asked him if he needed a hug. He did indeed, and in truth, so did I.

ↄ

Guy Claxton, from The Unknown Region: Inspirations on Living and Dying:

There is a Sufi story about a man who was walking in the market place one afternoon when someone tugged at his sleeve. "I am Death," said the figure. "I just came to warn you that we have an appointment at six o'clock tomorrow morning."

The man was very scared, but he thought he would make good use of the advance information. Cashing in his shares, he bought the three finest, fastest horses in the town, and he set off across the desert to a distant town where he hoped Death would not be able to find him. All night he rode like the wind, exhausting one horse after the other, until, as six o'clock approached, he came to a small oasis where he dismounted for a quick drink before continuing.

As he walked over to the well, the figure that had been sitting quietly beside it looked at his watch and stood up saying, "It's remarkable. I really didn't think you were going to be able to make it!" As we become, or think we become, nearer to death, the value of time and relationships increases immensely. We can all learn from those who look at death.

ↄ

Different cultures deal with and perceive death differently. Western versus Eastern

Avoid death vs. Prepare for it
Fight it vs. Accept it
It's the end vs. It is part of the cycle

ↄ

Interesting Euphemisms for Death (Authors Unknown)

Taking a dirt nap.

She's gone to where the old people go after Florida.

A person's heavenly birthday.

Lost his fight with entropy (decline into disorder).

Leaving the Sample (statistics).

Patient will be discharged to the 8th floor (hospital has 7 floors).

Ambulance term: DRT = Dead right there.

He's eating grass by the roots.

Gone to the other side of the mirror.

☙

I'm not there! (?)

Don't cry at my grave
'Cause I won't be there
I'll be in the breeze
That ruffles in your hair.

I'll be in the sunshine
I'll be in the snow
I'll be in the places
Where we used to go.

I'll be in your laughter
And in funny things
I'll be in your shadow
And there in your dreams.

I'll be in your greeting
But not your goodbyes
I'll be in the reflection
Of your loving eyes.

I'll always be with you
And I'll always care
So don't cry at my graveside
'Cause I won't be there.

☙

Akeela Bee

We ask ourselves: Who am I to be brilliant, gorgeous, talented, and fabulous?

Actually, who are we not to be?

We are born to make manifest the glory of the "God" that is within us, and as we let our own light shine, we unconsciously give others permission to do the same.

☙

Rich Couple Give Up Lives, So Others Can Receive
Laura Baenen (AP)

MINNEAPOLIS – The day Richard and Helen Brown were found dead in their garage; letters of explanation began arriving in their friends' mailboxes. The ailing, elderly couple had chosen suicide so they could leave their entire $10 million fortune to charity, rather than spend some of it on medical treatment.

"They were taking the high road to death," their former pastor, Charles Heuser, said Monday. The Browns, married 53 years, had made their money in radio stations and from a broadcasting school they founded..

In recent months, Richard Brown, 79, had to use a wheelchair because of arthritis and asthma. Helen Brown, 76, had Alzheimer's disease. Both had polio as children.

The Browns' bodies were found Dec. 5 in their Cadillac Eldorado in the garage of their Fort Lauderdale, Florida retirement home. Both died of carbon monoxide poisoning. Their will specified that their money should go to United Church of Christ organizations. "We have the means to afford the best doctors, hospitals and around-the-clock home care to the end of our lives, but neither of us wants that kind of life," the Browns wrote in letters that began arriving Dec. 5. "It would also consume a substantial part of our money, which through our will and through the mission work of our church is destined to help many young people throughout the world who may one day be able to help many more.

"We have no immediate family or heirs. In a sense, this legacy represents the final purpose of our lives."

"To them, it would be a poor use of money" to spend it on care for their deteriorating bodies, "said Heuser, who had advised them to leave their wealth to United Church of Christ missions. Heuser of Gold Beach, Ore., said he did not know they would commit suicide but that he could not fault them for doing so. The Rev. Dave Hohmann, who will preside at a memorial service Thursday, said their religion teaches against passing judgment on people who committed suicide. Our job is to remember the good," Hohmann said.

And there are many who recalled the Browns' kindness'. Connie Wester, a secretary at the broadcasting school, recalled Richard Brown's reaction when Wester and her husband adopted a baby.

"Mr. B wanted me to determine whether I wanted to be a full-time mother," she said. "So he gave me a month off with pay and said I was welcome to come back but said he would understand if I wanted to be home full time. That was pretty special that he would do that."

Wester, who still works at the National Education Center – Brown Institute campus, was among several people who received the farewell note from the Browns. It arrived at home when she was at work. "It was extremely emotional. My daughter read it to me over the phone. She was crying and I was crying. It's very hard to know they're never coming back."

The Browns founded the American Institute of the Air in Minneapolis in 1946 with money they made selling a few small stations in Minnesota. The school, renamed Brown Institute, was sold to CBS in 1972, and the Browns continued to run it until 1982. CBS later sold it to National Education Centers. His health deteriorating, Brown moved his wife in the early 1980's to Fort Lauderdale, where they had started another small broadcast school.

Don Stoner, director of planned giving for the United Church of Christ in Cleveland, said he met with the Browns two weeks ago as they completed their wills. "They were concerned about how funds would be wisely and prudently managed, how their money would have the most impact," Stoner said. He said he and another church official at the meeting had no idea what the Browns were planning. Then they received the letters. "It knocked the socks off the both of us," Stoner said.

⁂

Mother Lays Down Her Life for Sake of Life-to-Be
Anna Borgman (Washington Post)

WASHINGTON – Clemintina Geraci, three months pregnant, made the decision of her life when doctors told her last spring that her breast cancer had spread. She could fight the cancer aggressively and have an abortion, or she could take less hazardous cancer drugs and carry the baby to term.

Four months ago, she gave birth to Dylan Geraci Winn. And Saturday Dylan, wearing a light blue knit jumper, slept peacefully at his mother's funeral. A black beret on her balding head, Geraci spent the best of her final days at the hospital and her home in Riverdale, Md., holding Dylan and making videotapes for him to watch as he grows up. The steroids had distorted her face and body, but she wanted her son to know who she was and who she had been. On the tapes, Geraci told him about his Italian grandparents, about her favorite music, about her dreams for him. And she read bedtime stories, including Dr. Seuss' Green Eggs and Ham.

Time ran out before she could get to The Velveteen Rabbit.

Geraci, died Monday, March 6, at Washington Hospital Center, where she had worked as a resident in obstetrics and gynecology. She was 34. "She didn't win, but she forced death to change its terms," said Pierre Tooele, Dylan's godfather. "She died with dignity."

More than 100 friends and family members gathered at the Unitarian Universalist Church of Silver Spring, Md., to remember her Saturday. They described a strong, vivacious, passionate woman who lived her life with integrity, loved music and cooked a mean marinara sauce. "She was a stereotypical fiery Italian," said her husband, David Winn, a resident at George Washington University Medical Center in Washington, D.C.

Geraci was diagnosed with breast cancer two years ago when she asked to have a mammogram. Routine self exams had not detected a lump, but Geraci's mother had died from the disease, and she wanted to be careful. She had a mastectomy, and doctors told her that the cancer appeared to be gone. They advised her to wait six months before getting pregnant, although no one knew if the chemotherapy might make her sterile. After getting the all clear, she did become pregnant.

Then Geraci started seeing spots and having blurry vision. The cancer had spread to a lung and an eye. By the time she gave birth, it had metastasized throughout her spine, liver and brain.

"We all understood what (chemotherapy choice) meant," said obstetrician Oscar Mims, who delivered Dylan. "They were two people in love who made a conscious decision to have a baby.

Who was I to say otherwise? They were both physicians and clearly understood the options."

Phillip Goldstein, chief of obstetrics and gynecology at Washington Hospital Center, said "Geraci's death has been a trial. It's not fair to have a young person die," Goldstein said, his voice cracking. "I rage about the death of such a valuable human being."

But he expected nothing else from Geraci. "It wasn't because she was pro-life," he said. "It was because it was the right thing for her to do."

During most of her pregnancy, Geraci took taxol, which doctors thought would not harm Dylan. She had to stop taking the drug during the seventh month of pregnancy, and Dylan was born one month prematurely by Cesarean section, during which doctors discovered cancer in her liver. She resumed treatment, but it was too late.

Geraci was born in Italy and grew up in poverty in Wethersfield, Conn., said longtime friend Diane Kaplan, a psychologist and Dylan's godmother. She was spiritual but not religious, Kaplan said, and only recently began attending services at the Unitarian church. "Even if she had ended the pregnancy, there was no guarantee she could treat the cancer," Kaplan said. "It was a goal of her life to have a child. She really saw this as her one chance. She was a risk-taker. She was hoping to be able to beat the cancer, too. We all roll the dice in our own way."

☙

In my opinion, the feeling of LOSS following death is perfectly described by this poem:
Stop all the clocks, cut off the telephone,
prevent the dog from barking with a juicy bone,
silence the pianos and with muffled drum
bring out the coffin, let the mourners come.

Let airplanes circle moaning overhead
scribbling on the sky the message He is dead,
put crepe bows round the white necks of the public doves,
let the traffic policemen wear black cotton gloves.

He was my North, my South, my East and West,

my working week and my Sunday rest,
my noon, my midnight, my talk, my song;
I thought that love would last forever; I was wrong.

The stars are not wanted now; put out every one;
pack up the moon and dismantle the sun;
pour away the ocean and sweep up the wood;
for nothing now can ever come to any good.

APRIL 1936, FROM W.H. AUDEN COLLECTED POEMS

༄

"Candle in the Wind," November to December, 1991

Claude Jutra, filmmaker and sufferer of Alzheimer's disease, discussing the disorientation with John Hofsess, The conversations occurred a few months before Jutra committed suicide, 5 Nov. 1986, by leaping off Montreal's Jacques Cartier Bridge. "I can face death, but I cannot face watching myself disappear from within. Nowadays, when the world comes knocking at the door of Claude Jutra, there's no one home. I don't know who I am anymore."

༄

Northrop Frye, The Double Vision: Language and Meaning in Religion

"The Spirit of creation who brought life out of chaos brought death out of it too, for death is all that makes sense of life in time. The Spirit that broods on the chaos of our psyches brings to birth a body that is in time and history but not enclosed by them, and is in death only because it is in the midst of life as well."

༄

Jan Crispin, physician concerned with alternative medicine, and Heather Phillip, PhD.

"Beyond Beneficence: An Ethical Perspective on Terminal Care," Humane Medicine, Nov. 1987. "Because the ethos of our culture is so deeply pervaded by materialism, by the priority of material well-being, we experience a collective need to preserve the appearance of happiness. Real death, real grief, is no longer acknowledged in the collective public awareness."

༄

**Gary Lautens, columnist and humorist,
The Toronto Star, 2 Feb. 1992.**

"When I croak, Eldon will not be chiseled into my tombstone. I refuse to pay for something I didn't use while living." Gary Eldon Lautens, who never used his middle name, wrote a column about the subject on Friday; he died unexpectedly on Saturday; the column appeared alongside tributes and obituary on Sunday."

ღ

**Speech of the lawyer in Morley Torgov's novel
St. Farb's Day (1990)**

"People come and go on the face of the earth. They grow, get cut down and disposed of, like grass. All that any human being can possibly claim and enjoy is a short-term lease, even when his lawyer hands him a fancy piece of paper with a great big seal on it called 'a deed.' Death notices are nothing more than lists of expired leases. We're all tenants here, even when we call ourselves landlords. Property appreciates. Man? Man simply depreciates."

ღ

**Michael Ignatieff,
The Needs of Strangers (1985)**

"We have needs of the spirit because we are the only species whose fate is not simply a mute fact of our existence but a problem whose meaning we attempt to understand."

ღ

Sue Rodriguez, Victim of ALS

"I want to ask you gentlemen, if I cannot give consent to my own death, then whose body is this? Who owns my life?" (amyotrophic lateral sclerosis, Lou Gehrig's disease, a terminal illness), appearing in a videotaped presentation to a Commons' subcommittee in Nov. 1992 in which she urged amendments to the section of the Criminal Code that makes it a crime for any person to assist another's suicide; quoted by Deborah Wilson in The Globe and Mail, 5 Dec. 1992.

ღ

Maurus E. Mallon, aphorist, 2 May 1993

"If, as Schopenhauer claims, each farewell is a preparation for death, then every greeting is an affirmation of life."

※

Robin Skelton, poet and aphorist,
A Devious Dictionary (1991).

"Death is the only mystery we all solve."

※

Roderick Haig Brown, author and angler,
A River Never Sleeps

"I should think there is nothing very bad about dying expect for the people one has to leave and the things one hasn't had time to do. When the time comes, if I know what it's all about, I suppose I shall think, among other things, of the fish I haven't caught and the places I haven't fished."

※

Robertson Davies, novelist,
interviewed by Tom Harpur in 1975.

"One of the things that puzzles me is that so few people want to look at life as a totality and to recognize that death is no more extraordinary than birth." Conversations with Robert Davies (1989) edited by J. Madison Davis.

※

This was taken from the wall of a wonderful bar, Latitude 22, in Cabo San Lucas. The feeling of tight comradeship was evident everywhere. I'm sure there are many places where this feeling resides, where friends with common interests gather.

In Memory of Danny Crespi:

Another golden sunset melts into the sea
Bringing back a memory of a place we used to be
Those last few fading moments, before the sun has gone
Down along the waterfront, we'll hear your footsteps come
Reminds us of our time with you, so short but yet so long

Your gentle disposition, your face, familiar smile
We cannot help but take the time and think of you a while
If no man is an island, then you will never be alone
Our thoughts are always with you,
Our hearts will be your home
Set sail now on your voyage
Wherever that may be
You'll always be the captain
The Danny we remember from the Sea
5-22-94

∞

After reading newspapers from around the country, I have seen distinct obituary topics. These were fairly consistent when written by others. General themes were:

YOUNG

After reading children's obituaries it became clear to me that we would all feel more alive if we lived as children do…to the fullest

OLD

I see a few warm and wonderful stories about old people, or else there is no story at all. As if they outlived those who knew them. All the more reason to write your own.

LOVED AND WAS LOVED

Many cared about this person. He/she was an important part of many lives and spent energy to impact people positively.

GRATITUDE

These people gave credit and thanks to those who provided valuable service and love in the final days or months of life.

EDUCATION

Was a great influence; this life touched others by example, knowledge and experience. Results were created by this person's actions,

PERSONAL REFLECTIONS

Special words and/or ideas, which were important to this person, often reflecting their core values or character.

ENJOYED ACTIVITIES

Sports, gardening, sewing, reading, writing, movies, camping, anything that increased enjoyment for this person and those associated with him.

WORK

This person's life was his/her work. Their work described whom they were...sometimes fulfilling, sometimes not.

MEMBERSHIP

It was important to this person to be a part of a larger group, sharing ideas and work to accomplish more than one person could.

ACHIEVEMENT

Paper and plaques mark this person's life. Recognition came in many areas, i.e. work, games, charity, military scholastics. Most touching were the personal achievements.

CAUSE OF DEATH

Terminal illness, accidents, or other cause of death were the primary subject.

REGRETS

Many obituaries contain statements of expressed unresolved problems, unkept promises or unspoken words.

CONCLUSION

A friend of mine once owned a bookstore. She occasionally had authors presenting their "wares" to groups at her store. I have imagined myself in front of such a group. What would I say? What would I be thinking? Why am I here?

I'm here because I had an idea that hauled me away. I've been happy about that. As it has expanded to those around me its value has grown for them and me. I thought I was looking at my death when in fact it was about my life.

Obituaries are about lives of people no longer here. I'm sorry I didn't know them a little better, I'm sorry we all didn't. After reading literally volumes of obituaries, I found it interesting that no one wrote: so-and-so had the biggest house, was the best dressed, never made a mistake, things we seem to take so seriously every day.

When you truly pay attention to obituaries you see value coming from family, friends, work associates, etc. If we can believe the words of dying people, lasting value seems to come from experiences and emotions. There is certainly more to gain from this experience than a piece for the paper. It has been said in many ways: for life to be all that it can be, it must be lived, must be spent. I like the idea of not just living the length of life but also the breadth. I believe writing your own obituary will help achieve this.

The actual time of a person's death is difficult enough. It is a difficult time to reflect on the "real" life of a person. Some may think writing one's own obituary is self-centered or narcissistic, but no one is more qualified to accurately portray your life than you.

I'd like to be so bold as to say what I want: I want everyone who encounters this idea to at least be open enough to spend one half hour of their lives writing their own obituary. Once it's done keep it handy. It will, more than likely, change. I encourage you to wait not a minute longer. Ideas about your life are in your mind right now. Say what is important to you. Share your true self. Life entails risk, but the biggest risk of all is dying without having lived. Use your obituary to say how you would like your life to be (or have been). If you like the idea of a retreat designed around writing your own please let me know. Remember, I'd very much like to receive a copy.

Good Living,

Craig

ACKNOWLEDGMENTS

It's odd. When we die it is just us dying. There may be others around, but it is our singular act. No one can do it for us, although they can do it to us.

That being said, we mostly accomplish things in life with help. I had some, and I want to acknowledge those people. First, Cheryl Defa for writing hers so very long ago.

My wife Mitzi, children Erin and Miles were always in my heart while I was writing and collecting. I realized how much I was going to miss them.

My English teacher gave up hope for me a long time ago. I want to personally thank Kat Majors for fixing my many gramatical (that's right I misspelled grammatical), and punctuation errors.

In the "last but not least" department this project would still be stuck on my computer were it not for the energy and talent of my very good and talented friend, Martha Cowen, editor, chief and spark plug.

RELATED READING

Aries, Philippe. **The Hour of Our Death.**
New York: Knopf. 1981

Arya, Usharbudh Pandit. **Meditation and the Art of Dying.** Honesdale, PA.: Himalayan Publishers. 1979

Becker, Ernst. **The Denial of Death.**
New York: Hobbs, Dorman, 1971

Boerstler, Richard. **Letting Go: A Holistic and Meditative Approach to Living and Dying.** South Yarmouth, MA: Associates in Thanatology. 1982

Callanan, Maggie. **Final Gifts.** New York: Poseidon Press, 1992

Campbell, Joseph. **The Masks of God.**
New York: Viking Press, 1968

Camath, M. V. **Philosophy of Death and Dying.**
Honesdale, PA: Himalayan Publishers. 1978

Chaney, Earlyne. **The Mystery of Death and Dying: Initiation at the Moment of Death.** York Beach, ME: Samuel Weiser. 1988

Duda, Deborah. **Coming Home: A Guide to Dying at Home with Dignity.** Santa Fe, NM: Aurora Press, 1987

Foos–Graber, Anya. **Deathing.** York Beach, Maine: Nicolas – Hays. 1989

Free John, Da. **Easy Death: Talks and Essays on the Inherent and Ultimate Transcendence of Death and Everything Else.** San Raphael, CA: Dawn Horse, 1983

Killiam–Wilber, Treya. **Grace and Grit.**
Boston/London: Shambhala, 1993

Kubler–Ross, Elisabeth. **On Death and Death and Dying.** New York: MacMillan Publishing, 1969

Kubler–Ross, Elisabeth. **Death, The Final Stage of Growth.** Englewood Cliffs, NJ: Prentice – Hall. 1979

Levine, Steven. **Who Dies: An Investigation of Conscious Living and Conscious Dying.** New York: Doubleday. 1982

Nuland, Sherwin B. **How We Die.** New York: Knopf. 1994

Rinpoche, Sogyal. **The Tibetan Book of Living and Dying.** San Francisco: Harpers, 1992

RELATED VIDEOS

Death: The Trip of a Lifetime. A KCTS Television & Palmer/Fenster Inc. Co. production, in association with Stoner Productions. Distributed by: Ambrose Video Publishing, Inc., 1290 Avenue of the Americas, Suite 2245 New York, N.Y. 10104

Conversations on the Edge: On Death and Healing and the Spirit. Distributed by: I.S.H.I. Box 316 Bolinas, CA. 94924 Phone (415) 868-2642

INTERNET

www.wikipedia.com

www.mywonderfullife.com

www.whowritesforyou.com

www.affinitycremation.com

www.celestis.com

www.lifegem.com

www.funeralsite.com

www.kuhnfuneralhome.com

The Last Lecture by Randy Paush, www.thelastlecture.com

Funeral Homes

Diamond

www.eHow.com

Home Page for DeathNet:
http://www.u.arizona.edu/~gwj/Deathnet.htm

Newsgroup: news: alt.obituaries

My Email: craigdunford@yahoo.com

www.ingramcontent.com/pod-product-compliance
Lightning Source LLC
Chambersburg PA
CBHW051808040426
42446CB00007B/572